A Comparative Survey of Historical and Contemporary Slavery

Unfinished Business:
A Comparative Survey of Historical and Contemporary Slavery

Joel Quirk

Wilberforce Institute for the study of
Slavery and Emancipation
University of Hull

Published in 2009 by the United Nations Educational,
Scientific and Cultural Organization
7, place de Fontenoy, 75352 Paris 07 SP, France

Coordination and contact
The Slave Route Project
Division of Cultural Policies and Intercultural Dialogue
UNESCO, 1, rue Miollis, 75732 Paris Cedex 15 – France
Tel: (33)1 45 68 49 45
www.unesco.org/culture/slaveroute

Wilberforce Institute for the study of Slavery and Emancipation
Oriel Chambers
27 High Street
HU1 1NE, United Kingdom.
Contact: wise@hull.ac.uk
http://www.hull.ac.uk/wise/

ISBN 978-92-3-104124-2

Photographs
p. 17, right © UNESCO/Becka, M.
p. 23, right © UNESCO.
p. 35, right © UNESCO.
p. 51, right, © UNESCO/Loock, F.
p. 73, right, © UNESCO/Roger, D.
p. 93, left, © UNESCO; right, © UNESCO/Malempré, G.
p. 113, right, © UNESCO/ Sopova, J.

The ideas and opinions expressed in this publication are those of
the authors and are not necessarily those of UNESCO and do not
commit the Organization.

The designations employed and the presentation of material
throughout this publication do not imply the expression of any
opinion whatsoever on the part of UNESCO concerning the legal
status of any country, territory, city or area or of its authorities or
concerning the delimitation of its frontiers or boundaries.

Graphic design and typesetting:
Soledad Munoz Gouet – solemg@free.fr
Printed by Laballery - 907096

Printed in France

About the Author

Dr Joel Quirk is the Deputy Director of the Wilberforce Institute for the study of Slavery and Emancipation (WISE), University of Hull. His research primarily focuses upon the historical relationship between the legal abolition of slavery and contemporary forms of human bondage. This is reflected in a forthcoming book entitled *The Anti-Slavery Project: Bridging the Historical and Contemporary* (University of Pennsylvania Press). Joel's work has also recently been published in *Human Rights Quarterly*, *The Journal of Human Rights*, *Review of International Studies*, *The International Journal of Human Rights*, *The Journal of Modern European History*, and *The Oxford Handbook of International Relations*.

About WISE

The Wilberforce Institute for the study of Slavery and Emancipation (WISE) is dedicated to the pursuit of world class research in the areas of slavery, emancipation, human rights, and social justice. The institute seeks to improve knowledge and understanding of both historical practices and contemporary problems, and to inform public policy and political activism. As part of this agenda, the institute is currently engaged in extensive research into modern forms of slavery, including specific projects focusing upon the exploitation of migrants in the United Kingdom, forced marriage practices and human trafficking, repairing historical wrongs, the regulation of global supply chains and business ethics, the global parameters of child slavery, modern slavery in the Indian subcontinent, and migration and exploitation in sub-Saharan Africa. These projects build upon a series of recent conferences and a range of local and international partnerships. For information about these projects, please consult www.hull.ac.uk/wise/, or email Joel Quirk at j.quirk@hull.ac.uk.

About UNESCO's *Slave Route* Project

Well aware that ignoring or attempting to hide key historic events can become an obstacle to mutual understanding, international reconciliation and stability, UNESCO decided to raise international awareness on the slave trade and slavery as a means of contributing to the preservation of peace. Humanity's collective conscience must not forget this tragedy, symbolizing the denial of the most basic human rights. By virtue of its scale, its duration and the violence that characterized it, the slave trade is regarded as the greatest tragedy in human history. Moreover, it has caused profound transformations, which account in part for a large number of geopolitical and socio-economic changes that have shaped today's world. It also raises some of the most burning contemporary issues e.g., racism, cultural pluralism, construction of new identities and citizenship.

The Slave Route Project was officially launched in 1994 in Ouidah, Benin. The concept of "route" was chosen to illustrate the flow of exchanges among peoples, cultures and civilizations that has influenced societies worldwide. In addition to exploring the historical aspects of slavery, the project aims to improve understanding of the present and to contribute to the current debate regarding multi-ethnic and multicultural societies.

The main objectives of the Slave Route Project are: to contribute to a better understanding of the slave trade, its processes and implications, through multidisciplinary research; to objectively highlight the consequences of the slave trade on modern societies, in particular the global transformations and cultural interactions among peoples generated by the tragedy; and to contribute to the establishment of a culture of tolerance and peaceful coexistence between peoples by encouraging intercultural dialogue.

Since its inception, the project has been organized around five closely linked programmes in various fields of activity, including scientific research, the development of pedagogic tools, the collection and preservation of written archives and oral traditions, inventorying and preserving places and sites of memory related to slavery, the promotion of intangible artistic and spiritual expressions derived from slavery and slave trade; and the contributions of the African Diaspora.

For further information on the objectives and activities of the UNESCO Slave Route Project, consult :

http://portal.unesco.org/culture/en/ev.php-URL_ID=25659&URL_DO=DO_TOPIC&URL_SECTION=201.html

This project has greatly benefited from important contributions from Anna Rajander, David Richardson, Douglas Hamilton, Edmond Moukala, Judith Spicksley, Kevin Bales, Mick Wilkinson, Nicholas Evans, and Saori Terada.

Preface to Unfinished Business:
Five Themes of Failure

Kevin Bales

When George Santayana wrote that 'Those who cannot remember the past are condemned to repeat it,' did he guess that it would become an empty mantra often repeated by exactly those people about to live out the doom of their historical ignorance? Perhaps Santayana's aphorism was just too pithy, too close to a modern sound-bite, so that his words are echoed but not grasped. In our response to contemporary forms of slavery, Santayana's words are prophetic, and frame the importance of Joel Quirk's *Unfinished Business*.

By my reckoning we are embarked upon the fourth major anti-slavery movement in human history. Each of these movements sought the common goal of liberation for slaves; each of them has been also beset and delayed by fights over numbers, definitions, and the appropriation of slavery as a stalking horse for other political or ideological goals. Each of these movements has had its energy and resources wasted in schism and duplication, often breaking along the same lines as the previous movement decades before. All have needed a greater understanding of the recurring problems that have an impact on social reform movements, whatever their aim. Taking a broad view of the current global anti-slavery movement, while recognizing its many successes, I want to point to five themes of failure. These are themes repeated with the ineluctable regularity of Greek tragedy across all previous anti-slavery movements and which continue to plague us today. They are fervour; dilution; co-optation; ego-driven leadership; and the mixed bag of government involvement.

Fervour It may seem strange to point to fervour or enthusiasm as a problem. Doesn't every movement need a strong emotional involvement as motivation? Obviously, no anti-slavery campaign could have been sustained without the great power of individuals deeply moved and called to bring their lives and fortunes into the struggle. The problem occurs not in the awakening of minds and hearts to the horrors of slavery and the duty of liberation, but when those so changed and convinced are never helped to grow into thoughtful, effective abolitionists. Outrage is a reasonable initial response to the fact of slavery, but it is not a sustainable strategy for its eradication. Today, sadly, there is a tendency to make slavery simple, to portray this complex social and economic relationship as an issue in black and white, of good versus evil. The result is a call for quick, simple answers and worse: an assumption that being morally right transcends the need for truth or logic. It is an assumption that ignores cultures and contexts that are essential facts of slavery. One of the key reasons why constant debate surrounds the numbers of people in slavery is that many estimates are assertions based on outrage rather than analysis. Fervour can overcome logic, and is unaffected by the realities where slavery is actually being combated. One example will suffice: Slave labour in cocoa farming in Côte d'Ivoire was exposed in 2001. Some years later a British group began campaigning for boycotts of cocoa products. In their published reports and interviews they asserted that 'A 2002 [ILO] study estimated that at least 284,000 children were trapped in forced labour in the West African cocoa industry, the majority of these – some 200,000 – were to be found in Ivory Coast.' Yet, the ILO report actually said nothing of the sort, stating instead that '284,000 children are estimated to be employed in child labour in Cameroon, Côte d'Ivoire, Ghana, and Nigeria (i.e. not just in cocoa).' This group also stated that 'the number of chocolate slaves is at least 12,000'. Yet, when traced to its source, the actual reference read '12,000 of the child labourers had no relatives in the area, suggesting they were trafficked'. Yes, it is easier to raise funds, recruit supporters, and make headlines when facts are simplified or fabricated, but such a smokescreen of obfuscation, however well meant, only serves to blind us to the right road to liberation. As is the case with all five themes of failure, such fervour also generates schism within the anti-slavery movement as those groups most convinced of their moral purity are least likely to participate in the give and take of collective decision-making. Our fervour needs to lead us toward deeper involvement in complex realities rather than toward simplification. These realities are challenging. For example, we need to understand the processes through which child slaves in fishing sometimes become slaveholding fishermen themselves, or the cyclical self-reinforcing processes of forced prostitution, through which brutalized victims can in some cases eventually become sex traffickers.

2. *Dilution –* When anti-slavery work was aimed at the abolition of legal slavery it was relatively easy not to lose sight of either who was in slavery or the desired goal. Slaves were those caught in legal slavery, the desired end was the abolition of that legal

status; but when that simplicity was lost in the first anti-slavery victories, a dilution of key concepts began to threaten the direction of abolitionist work. For example, the abolition of legal slavery in most parts of the British Empire in 1833 also required a five-year period of 'forced apprenticeship' for freed slaves. Researchers from the Anti-Slavery Society soon determined that this apprenticeship had all the violent and exploitive characteristics of previously legal slavery, but found it difficult to mobilize public opinion around an issue that was now seen as solved. In that case, real slavery was hidden behind another name. Today it is equally likely that something that is not slavery will hide behind that name. Without the easy yardstick of a legal definition any group seeking to dramatize its issue can appropriate the word 'slavery'. Discussing the UN Working Group, Joel Quirk puts it well when he states that 'slavery has arguably come to be little more than short-hand for virtually any form of severe ill-treatment and exploitation'. The problem becomes even more acute when we look to the popular media and public discourse. Here we find 'shopping slaves', 'slaves to fashion', and pop-idol Britney Spears singing 'I'm a slave 4 U' – none of which have anything to do with the violent expropriation of labour. One reason that raising public awareness of contemporary slavery is challenging is that the word 'slavery' must be first reclaimed and reinvested with its actual meaning. Around the edges of the contemporary anti-slavery movement are also those groups who would believe they would benefit from stretching the meaning of the word 'slavery' to include such issues as all forms of prostitution, incest, all forms of child labour, all prison labour, and the coercive mental control exercised by television. The result is that the dilution of meaning leads to a dilution of effort with schismatic effect. I would assert that there are commonalities across all forms of slavery that set out its defining features: complete control of one person by another, violence and threat used to maintain that control, economic exploitation, and no payment beyond subsistence. This is a working definition that allows the movement to maintain its focus.

Co-optation – That last example of stretching the meaning of 'slavery' to include other phenomena can also be used in the process of co-opting the anti-slavery movement by other issues, groups, ideological or political campaigns. It is well understood how nineteenth century campaigns for slave emancipation became vehicles for women's emancipation efforts, a natural but distinct outgrowth. In the twenty-first century anti-slavery efforts can also mask other aims. Often those groups seeking to use anti-slavery work to further their own agenda will, as discussed above under *fervour*, simplify and reduce the issue, thus making it easier to manipulate and control. Some Evangelical Christian groups have been especially prone to this throughout all four of the global anti-slavery movements. Some have offered the quick and appealing option of simply buying slaves in order to set them free, others call for knee-jerk boycotts of products that, if realized, would actually push poor farmers into destitution and, potentially, enslavement. Opponents of the out-sourcing of jobs from the rich North to the developing world will state that these new jobs are 'slavery'. Those that call for the abolition of prostitution sometimes equate this demand to that of freedom for slaves. All of these dilute the concept of slavery, but it is the decision to then appropriate and exploit the term that carries this into co-optation. The result is that the abolition of slavery becomes one more plank of a larger ideological platform, thus alienating potential supporters that may not subscribe to that ideology. Since 2000 the battle over slavery and human trafficking in the United States has been very much a battle for ownership of the issue by political groups, and rather less a struggle to find the most effective ways to achieve abolition. In the public religious discourse it is hard not to get the impression that the issue belongs not to all citizens, but primarily to those who subscribe to a specific Evangelical Christianity. While nearly all of these groups preach inclusion, they tend to practice exclusion, with the result that schisms form and resources and energies are wasted. Finally, there is another theme repeated today that stretches back into the nineteenth century: anti-Muslim prejudice operating under the cloak of anti-slavery campaigning. While some have been involved in slavery (as have all religious traditions), Muslims have been especially targeted by some European and American groups for denunciation in ways that seem to have more to do with religious origin than their role in global slavery.

Ego-driven leadership – This is hardly a characteristic unique to anti-slavery movements, nearly every social movement has either benefited from good altruistic leaders, suffered under ego-driven leaders, or experienced both. All three of the previous anti-slavery movements began with visionary individuals who were often difficult human beings. There are many good leaders in the global anti-slavery movement, but there are two types of leaders that create the potential for failure – those that have given in to outrage, and those whose interests are self-serving. The first group has been common in emergent anti-slavery movements. Faced with public ignorance and indifference many leaders crossed the line into dogmatism and rage. The more indifference they confronted, the more their rage grew. The more their rage grew, the more they were willing to sacrifice anything and anyone to the cause. The more they were willing to sacrifice, the more their own minds and the lives of those around them were damaged. The more they damaged themselves and others, the more they drove away the very people who could help the movement. Without the willingness to make sacrifices, it is difficult to move the mountains that must be moved, but how can a rational and efficient organization be built on the basis of rage, pain, paranoia, and crippling sacrifice? On the other hand are the opportunists that use anti-slavery work as a way to achieve their own aggrandizement and enrichment. Sadly, there are today some anti-slavery groups whose leadership maintains a rigid control, allows no financial transparency, suppresses the individual growth and development of workers, concentrates on media exposure instead of liberation and reintegration of slaves, and builds 'networks' of cronies and relatives. The result is often a superficial, carefully cultivated appearance of abolition that conceals a minimal impact upon the problem of slavery. Organizations with capacity to fund anti-slavery work, and the ability to publicly celebrate such work should be wary of building up the power of individual "heroes" at the expense of the more challenging work of building up the power of wider movements and groups of activists.

The Mixed Bag of Government Involvement On one hand the involvement of governments is the ultimate aim of much anti-slavery work. After all, when governments pass laws against slavery they are essentially promising their citizens that slavery will not be allowed within their borders. All nations have passed such laws, but enforcement lags far behind. In nearly every country around the world anti-slavery organizations are doing the work of governments, sometimes in face of governmental opposition. For national governments to devote resources and political will to the eradication of slavery is a great aspiration of the abolitionist movement. Yet, when governments do become involved, the results can be mixed and even counter-productive. In the most egregious cases some national governments use anti-slavery rhetoric as a screen behind which to conceal their policies of forced labour. Others, while ensuring the freedoms of their own citizens, allow the importation of large numbers of foreign women to be sexually exploited in their entertainment industries, while at the same time issuing policy documents against human trafficking. Much more common is the challenge faced when national governments place the greatest emphasis on apprehending and prosecuting slaveholders while the victims of trafficking and slavery have little or no assistance. It is difficult to name any country where governmental provisions for freed slaves carry them readily into autonomy and citizenship. And at the level of international diplomacy a final pattern emerges. Suzanne Miers' remarkable book *Slavery in the 20th Century*, demonstrates this clearly: whenever a country's national economic or diplomatic interests come into conflict with the aims of anti-slavery movements, national interests always take precedence.

I hope that this review of themes of failure within anti-slavery movements is not taken as a council of despair, but as an honest attempt to reflect upon failings as well as achievements. While some anti-slavery organizations have

12

suffered from one or more of these failings, it is also true that many have overcome such challenges and grown to be better and stronger actors against slavery. Nations such as Ghana and Brazil, making some of the first steps toward integrated and extensive anti-slavery programs, show us the way forward. And if the country of Mauritania follows through on its present commitments, it may be the first nation in history to attempt to build a fully developed plan for eradication of slavery within its borders. There is something evolving within the global anti-slavery movement because we are learning from mistakes. There is important emerging good practice – from knowing what is the right way to go about looking about people in slavery, and the most effective forms of reintegration of ex-slaves, but also about how to build resilience within communities that are resisting slavery. The spread of such good practices will lead to unpredictable but potentially amazing results. Today there is a very disparate global movement, and it is exciting to see what the next stage will be as networking and greater international cooperation occur. There are also intriguing new models that have never existed before, particularly in the area of business accountability, that have the potential to open entirely new areas of anti-slavery work. But little of this path ahead will be clear if we don't know where we came from. Illumination to understand that path follows in Joel Quirk's *Unfinished Business*.

Kevin Bales,
August 2008

Kevin Bales is President of Free the Slaves (www.freetheslaves.net), the US sister organization of Anti-Slavery International, and Visiting Professor at the Wilberforce Institute for the study of Slavery and Emancipation, University of Hull. His book *Disposable People: New Slavery in the Global Economy* was nominated for a Pulitzer Prize, and published in ten languages. Desmond Tutu called it "a well researched, scholarly and deeply disturbing expose of modern slavery". In 2006 his work was named one of the top "100 World-Changing Discoveries" by the association of British universities. He won the Premio Viareggio for services to humanity in 2000. The film based on his book, which he co-wrote, won a Peabody Award and two Emmy Awards. He was awarded the Laura Smith Davenport Human Rights Award in 2005; the Judith Sargeant Murray Award for Human Rights in 2004; and the Human Rights Award of the University of Alberta in 2003. He was a consultant to the UN Global Initiative to Fight Human Trafficking. Bales has advised the US, British, Irish, Norwegian, and Nepali governments, as well as the Economic Community of West African States (ECOWAS), on slavery and human trafficking policy. In 2005 he published *Understanding Global Slavery*. His book *Ending Slavery: How We Will Free Today's Slaves*, a roadmap for the global eradication of slavery, was published in Sept. 2007. He is currently editing a collection of modern slave narratives, and co-writing a book on slavery in the United States today with Ron Soodalter. He gained his Ph.D. at the London School of Economics.

Table of Contents

Unfinished Business

The history of slavery raises many uncomfortable political and moral questions. Until relatively recently, legal enslavement was widely regarded as a natural and all but inescapable feature of human existence, which appears to have been sanctioned, in one form or another, by every major civilization and religion. The key break with this enduring precedent occurred in the second half of the eighteenth century, with the emergence of an organized anti-slavery movement in some parts of Europe and the Americas. This fledgling movement would face tremendous political and economic obstacles. From the sixteenth century onwards, European traders had been supplying colonial settlements in the Americas with ever increasing numbers of slaves from Africa. This unprecedented investment in human bondage had proved to be a major commercial success, creating powerful vested interests that were heavily reliant upon slave labour. Over many decades, organized anti-slavery challenged this flourishing system on various fronts, leading to protracted contests over the status of slavery on both sides of the Atlantic. After numerous setbacks, false starts and a series of often violent conflicts, slavery was legally abolished throughout the Americas, with the final act coming with the passage of a 'Golden Law' abolishing slavery in Brazil.

The passing of Transatlantic slavery is often viewed as an historical endpoint, which relegated slavery to the distant past. This is misleading. Slavery remained legal in other parts of the globe well into the twentieth century, and in territories where slavery came to be legally abolished, human bondage and extreme exploitation regularly continued under other designations. Many governments would rush to declare that slavery was no longer a problem, but these declarations rarely matched events on the ground. In the immediate aftermath of legal abolition, this was chiefly a question of the widespread use of forced, bonded and indentured labour in many jurisdictions. Over the last half century, the primary focus has gradually shifted towards practices which are analogous to legal slavery, with human trafficking, sexual servitude and child labour acquiring particular prominence.

Interest in contemporary slavery has increased dramatically over the last ten years, but there remains a widespread tendency to view historical and contemporary slavery as independent fields of study. For most historians of slavery, current problems rarely enter into the picture, except perhaps as brief postscripts, which typically take the form of passing observations that the struggle against slavery has not entirely concluded. For those focused on the present, the bulk of whom are political activists and official agents, the history of slavery and abolition consistently takes a back seat to contemporary issues. While both approaches are perfectly legitimate and entirely understandable, they can indirectly foster an informal separation between past and present, which can obscure the historical roots of contemporary problems.

This book moves beyond this artificial divide, providing the first ever comparative survey of both historical practices and contemporary problems. In doing so, it draws upon a wide range of literatures and source materials. The primary goal here is not to provide a comprehensive account of a specific issue or event in the history of slavery, but instead to integrate some of the key findings of existing treatments of many different events within a broader historical and political perspective. By concentrating upon important parallels between past and present, the book offers new ways of engaging with many of the key relationships and connections that have shaped the historical trajectory of slavery and abolition over the last five centuries. It is also important to recognize, however, that the book also operates at a high level of generalization. This has meant that a number of important developments have been passed over, or sketched in relatively brief terms. These shortcomings are hard to avoid in a survey of this type, especially given the scale of the global issues involved, so it is important to approach the information presented here as an open invitation to further analysis, rather than the final word on any particular topic. To assist additional inquiries, the book also includes a substantial number of references, which provide information on many key sources and authors for readers seeking further information on specific issues.

The book is divided into five major chapters. The first chapter, 'Defining Slavery in all its Forms', examines a number of definitions of slavery, both past and present. When it comes to the history of slavery, the main task facing any definition of slavery is developing a formula which separates slavery from related forms of servitude. When it comes to contemporary slavery, the main task facing any definition of slavery is specifying which activities are sufficiently similar to legal slavery that they deserve to be placed on the same footing.

The second chapter, 'The Question of Numbers', examines a number of estimates of the scale of slavery, slave trading and other forms of human bondage. This starts with the history of Transatlantic slavery, where a great deal of information is available. This wealth of material is unusual. In most cases estimates of slave numbers are confined to informed extrapolations, which can often be complicated by the illegal nature of many of the practices involved.

The third chapter, 'Human Bondage in a Comparative Perspective', identifies a number of differences and similarities between historical and contemporary practices. Four main themes are identified here: i) demand, acquisition and control; ii) transit and transfer; iii) slave roles; and iv) slave resistance. These themes follow a loose sequence of events, with demand for slaves providing a basis for various modes of enslavement, market-driven migration, and a series of commercial exchanges. Once slaves reach their destination, we confront the further question of slave roles, which have been characterized by a range of economic, reproductive, military and social considerations. The final theme of this chapter is slave resistance, which applies to every stage in this complex chain. Slave resistance is commonly associated with overt acts such as rebellion, flight and suicide, but it can also extend to long-term efforts to develop autonomous spaces under extremely difficult circumstances. By considering each of these themes in turn, this chapter identifies a number of key differences and similarities between various historical and contemporary practices, paving the way for further analysis of the history of organized anti-slavery and contemporary activism.

The fourth chapter, 'Legal Abolition', starts by identifying three main paths through which the legal abolition of slavery has historically occurred. This finds expression in a series of brief case studies, starting with four countries which occupy key positions when it comes to the end of Transatlantic slavery; the United States of America, Saint Domingue/Haiti, Great Britain and Portugal. Each of these cases captures different aspects of a complex trajectory. The history of anti-slavery is often equated with social activism in Britain and the United States, but these countries are not representative of experiences elsewhere. These case studies are then followed by a survey of the history of the legal abolition of slavery in other parts of the globe, where anti-slavery measures were often closely connected with European imperialism and colonialism. This important relationship is explored through additional studies of the history of legal abolition of slavery in India, Nigeria, Ethiopia and Saudi Arabia.

The fifth chapter, 'Effective Emancipation', explores some of the key limitations of the legal abolition of slavery. Although slavery has been legally abolished throughout the world, the serious problems associated with slavery have continued to this day in various guises. Something more is required: effective emancipation. The chapter begins with the aftermath of legal abolition, which can be divided into short- and long-term dimensions. The immediate component is concerned with the widespread use of other forms of human bondage as an informal substitute for slavery following legal abolition. The long-term component is concerned with the enduring legacies of historical patterns of enslavement. The chapter then goes on to provide a further series of case studies of different aspects of contemporary slavery, focusing upon chattel slavery in Mauritania, debt-bondage in India, migrant domestic workers in Singapore, and human trafficking in Great Britain.

The conclusion of the book, 'Public Policy and Political Activism', outlines a series of general strategies and recommendations for addressing contemporary problems. This platform draws upon the key insights of previous chapters of the book, making a case for both targeted action and sweeping socioeconomic reform. This begins with four key themes: i) education, information and awareness; ii) further legal reform; iii) effective enforcement; and iv) release, rehabilitation and restitution. These four themes can be viewed as the core of anti-slavery activism, offering a targeted platform that should command support from across the political and ideological spectrum. It is also clear, however, that the fight against both contemporary slavery and the long-term legacies of historical slave systems requires systemic efforts to address larger socioeconomic problems. If we are serious about confronting contemporary slavery, we also need to be serious about larger questions of poverty, inequality, racism and discrimination.

The initial groundwork for this book was laid by Koïchiro Matsuura, Director-General of UNESCO, as part of preparations for the International Year to Commemorate the Struggle against Slavery and its Abolition in 2004. Building upon UNESCO's long-standing engagement with the study of slavery and abolition, most notably through the Slave Route Project, Koïchiro Matsuura declared that further inquiries into the history of slavery could be expected to play an important role in developing:

> an appropriate framework for the promotion of a fair dialogue between peoples with due regard for the universality of human rights and to confirm our commitment to combat all contemporary forms of slavery and racism (Matsuura, 2003).

This book forms part of this larger project. Not only does it seek to bring together a range of materials on many different aspects of slavery, both past and present; it also provides an innovative platform for promoting dialogue about ways of addressing both modern forms of slavery and the enduring legacies of historical slave systems.

Chapter One: Defining Slavery in all its Forms

Two main challenges have faced historical efforts to formulate a universal definition of slavery: i) developing a definition that captures key variations among a wide range of historical slave systems; and ii) developing a definition that consistently distinguishes between slavery and related forms of human bondage, such as serfdom, pawnship, debt-bondage and forced labour for the state. In this context, the most common approach has been to emphasize the nexus between property and treatment, with most attempts at historical definition classifying slavery in terms of a clearly defined legal status that would be distinguished from other institutions by the fact that individuals were classified as a species of property, or human chattel. This focus on property is conventionally understood in terms of a combination of largely unfettered authority and extreme treatment, with the exceptional degree of personalized control that masters exercised over their slaves going hand in hand with consistently high levels of institutionalized brutality, psychological abuse, and economic exploitation.

This familiar approach is evident in the definition of slavery enshrined in the Slavery, Servitude, Forced Labour and Similar Institutions and Practices Convention of 1926, which formally defined slavery as 'the status or condition of a person over whom any or all of the powers attaching to the right of ownership are exercised'. This key instrument was initially negotiated under the auspices of the League of Nations, and was later somewhat belatedly taken over by the United Nations in 1953. By 2002, there had been 95 ratifications, with parties accepting an obligation 'to prevent and suppress the slave trade' and '[t]o bring about, progressively and as soon as possible, the complete abolition of slavery in all its forms'. The word 'progressively' introduces a qualified commitment to gradual, rather than immediate reform. As we shall see in chapter four, this qualified formula reflects the fact that slavery remained an ongoing issue in a number of colonial jurisdictions during the 1920s. It is also worth noting that the 'forms' of slavery to be abolished were not made explicit. In the lead up to the Convention, several League bodies would identify a number of related practices, including chattel slavery, serfdom and debt bondage, but the Convention itself ultimately offers limited guidance on this crucial issue (Miers, 2003, pp. 101-133; Grant, 2005, pp. 159-166). In the face of this ambiguous situation, government officials have consistently interpreted the 1926 definition in highly restrictive terms, primarily confining its application to chattel slavery.

This widespread emphasis upon property remains open to a number of objections. According to a number of leading scholars of slavery, property provides an insufficient foundation for differentiating between slavery and other forms of servitude. This line of argument has been most eloquently expressed by Orlando Patterson. For Patterson, attempts to define slavery exclusively in terms of property are fundamentally misguided, since property claims can also apply to many other activities, including both serfdom and marriage practices. This challenge is directly applicable to the 1926 definition, which refers to 'any or all of the powers attaching to the right of ownership'. Viewed in purely procedural terms, a right of ownership can be logically extended well beyond familiar images of chattel slavery to include

24

well paid professional athletes, whose contracts are regularly bought and sold. One way of resolving this issue is to offer a more precise account of the rights involved, but this exercise is not as straightforward as it might first appear, since different historical slave systems often operated on quite different terms, making it difficult to formulate a general framework that effectively applies across cultural and historical lines.

Patterson favours a different solution to this dilemma, offering instead a sociological approach in which slavery is defined as 'the permanent, violent domination of natally alienated and generally dishonored persons' (Patterson, 1982, p. 13). This multi-faceted approach can be divided into three main strands: i) an exceptional level of personalized control, ii) social and genealogical isolation, and iii) distinctive forms of socio-political dishonour. For Patterson, slavery is as much a social as an interpersonal status, as interactions between master and slave are bound up in broader relations between slaves and societies. The key ingredient here is 'social death', where slavery is said to be defined by the social and institutional segregation of slaves within the prevailing political order, paving the way for severe forms of coercion and control.

[margin annotation: Patterson's definition]

[margin annotation: DEF'N 2]

This focus on the nexus between slavery, society and socialization is also echoed by Claude Meillassoux, who makes the important point that 'one captive does not make slavery'. For Meillassoux, slavery can be best understood as a far-reaching system which needed to be continually renewed through conflicts between different civilizations and cultures, with captured individuals being withdrawn from their native social milieu and gradually de-socialized and de-personalized, acquiring an 'alien' status within their new host society (Meillassoux, 1991, pp. 99-115). This formulation draws upon Meillassoux's expertise in West Africa, but is less applicable to societies that enslaved members of their own community, rather than external interlopers. This is not unusual. Definitions of slavery that are based on one set of historical experiences are often less suited to other settings. On this front, the main axis of contention has long been the imposition of an ethnocentric model of slavery chiefly based upon Transatlantic experiences upon other historical and cultural contexts.

[margin annotation: DEF'N 3 Meillassoux]

One prominent challenge to this widespread impulse comes from Igor Kopytoff and Suzanne Miers, who argue that 'Westerners considering 'slavery' in African societies must discard their own concepts of ownership, property, and the purchasing of people' (Kopytoff and Miers, 1977, p. 11). Kopytoff and Miers instead conclude that it is more appropriate to view slavery in terms of kinship, lineage, and 'rights-in-persons'. In this model, slavery in Africa can be situated within an elaborate social hierarchy, in which 'the kinsman, the adopted, the dependent, the client and the 'slave' abutted on one another and could merge into one another' (23). While there is no question that violence, exploitation and exclusion were essential to slavery in Africa, the context in which these activities took place does not fit neatly alongside more familiar Western models.

This line of argument has recently been taken up by Gwyn Campbell, who maintains that the history of slavery in many parts of India, Africa and Asia becomes clearer:

> if Western notions of a division of society into free and slave, and of slaves as property, are replaced with a vision of society as a hierarchy of dependency in which 'slaves' constituted one of a number of unfree groups from which menial labor was drawn to perform services both productive and nominally unproductive.

In such cases, it may be more appropriate to think in terms of:

> a reciprocal system in which obligations implied servitude to an individual with superior status, to a kin group or the crown, in return for protection (Campbell, 2004, pp. xxii-xxiii)

From this standpoint, the antithesis of slavery is not freedom, which can be associated with isolation and vulnerability, but advancement (personal or inter-generational) within an elaborate social hierarchy (see also Eaton, 2006, pp. 2-9; Patterson, 1991). While there is no question that these differences need to be analyzed and discussed, it is also important to keep their larger ramifications in perspective. On this front, it is worth emphasizing that historical differences between slave systems do not appear to have hampered frequent cross-cultural trading in slaves. This points to the presence of underlying similarities, as well as differences. It is also worth noting that definitional dilemmas are often much less of an issue once we focus our attention on specific historical cases, rather than slavery as a universal category. Most historians of slavery concentrate their energies upon the role of various issues and events that influenced the history of slavery at particular points in time. Within this case-specific approach it is often entirely reasonable to (sometimes cautiously) define slavery in relation to relevant sources, without entering abstract debates over universal definitions.

Most attempts at definition revolve around historical cases where slavery was a legal institution, but this approach is less suited to contemporary slavery, since slavery has now been formally abolished across the globe,

26

introducing a new set of analytical challenges. The main point at issue here has been an enduring divide between legal injunctions and substantive practices. If slavery has been legally prohibited, but its more heinous characteristics have continued under different designations, or through illicit activities, on what grounds can we say that slavery has effectively come to an end? If enslavement has continued to be a major problem in the absence of official recognition, on what grounds can we meaningfully distinguish slavery from similar forms of exploitation? In this environment, procedural distinctions between chattel slavery and analogous practices have become increasingly difficult to sustain.

This brings us back to the central concept of slavery *in all its forms*. It has long been recognized that chattel slavery shares many features in common with other forms of servitude. In the aftermath of legal abolition, these affinities have become increasingly important. Once we accept the basic proposition that abolition does not automatically translate into an effective end to slavery, we must also confront the more difficult task of specifying which activities are sufficiently similar to historical slave systems that they deserve to be placed on the same moral and legal footing. On this vital point, the sociological approach of Patterson, Meillassoux and others can offer limited guidance. If slavery is defined as a distinctive social system, rather than an individual affliction, few cases of modern bondage (no matter how heinous) formally amount to slavery.

Over the last half century the relationship between slavery and other forms of bondage has been gradually redefined. In this new formulation, chattel slavery is no longer conceived as a singular, exceptional category, but as one among many forms of 'contemporary' or 'modern' slavery. The main catalyst for this ongoing transformation has been the 1956 United Nations Supplementary Convention on the Abolition of Slavery, the Slave Trade, and Institutions and Practices Similar to Slavery. The key provisions of the Convention can be found in article one, which obligates parties to:

> take all practicable and necessary legislative and other measures to bring about progressively and as soon as possible the complete abolition or abandonment of the following institutions and practices, where they still exist and *whether or not they are covered by the definition of slavery contained in article 1 of the Slavery Convention signed at Geneva on 25 September 1926* (italics added).

In addition to chattel slavery, these obligations extend to four areas: debt bondage, serfdom, servile marriage, and the transfer of children for the purpose of exploitation.

These four practices are not explicitly classified as types of slavery, but are instead brought together under the amorphous category of persons of 'servile status'. Under the terms of the Convention, they are formally defined in the following terms:

> **(a)** Debt bondage, that is to say, the status or condition arising from a pledge by a debtor of his personal services or of those of a person under his control as security for a debt, if the value of those services as reasonably assessed is not applied towards the liquidation of the debt or the length and nature of those services are not respectively limited and defined;
>
> **(b)** Serfdom, that is to say, the condition or status of a tenant who is by law, custom or agreement bound to live and labour on land belonging to another person and to render some determinate service to such other person, whether for reward or not, and is not free to change his status;
>
> **(c)** Any institution or practice whereby: (i) A woman, without the right to refuse, is promised or given in marriage on payment of a consideration in money or in kind to her parents, guardian, family or any other person or group; or (ii) The husband of a woman, his family, or his clan, has the right to transfer her to another person for value received or otherwise; or (iii) A woman on the death of her husband is liable to be inherited by another person;
>
> **(d)** Any institution or practice whereby a child or young person under the age of 18 years, is delivered by either or both of his natural parents or by his guardian to another person, whether for reward or not, with a view to the exploitation of the child or young person or of his labour.

The inclusion of these practices within the Convention not only marked a major expansion in anti-slavery obligations under international law, it also endorsed a new understanding of the relationship between chattel slavery and other forms of bondage, placing slavery at the centre of a family of grievous human rights abuses.

More recent discussions of slavery have both expanded upon and further refined this underlying formula. Of particular significance here has been the work of the United Nations Working Group on Slavery, which first met in 1975 after protracted political manoeuvring. Faced with the difficult task of defining and demarcating slavery, the Group has instead adopted an open-ended approach. Over the years the Working Group has touched on a wide array of serious problems, from established issues such as chattel slavery, debt bondage, and servile marriage to larger concerns with genital mutilation, incest, honour killings and the sale of organs. This agenda not only involves a more expansive understanding of slavery, but also reflects ongoing efforts to repackage various political causes as species of slavery. In 1988 the Group was renamed the Working Group on Contemporary Forms of Slavery, which was held to be 'more descriptive of its actual interests, namely exploitation of sex, debt bondage, sale of children, *apartheid*'(United Nations, 1987, p. 26). The reference to apartheid stems from a 1966 debate within the United Nations, which established a formal connection between slavery and the 'slavery-like practices of apartheid and colonialism'. These practices would later be defined as 'forms of collective or group slavery that fundamentally oppress the human rights of several million people' (United Nations, 1982, p. 10). This inclusion signalled a further reconfiguration in the parameters of slavery by elevating collective burdens to the same status as individual afflictions.

A key component in this gradual redefinition has been the partial integration of a range of political agendas, as discussion of slavery has merged into discussion of related themes such as human rights, wartime abuses, child labour, state crime, sexual exploitation and human development. While many different issues can be raised here (see Bales, 2005; Bassiouni, 1991; Rassam, 1999; Weissbrodt et al., 2002; United Nations, 1951), there are three themes in particular that deserve to be highlighted: forced labour for the state, human trafficking and child labour. Forced labour has long been especially sensitive, because it revolves around direct compulsion under government direction. Its close connection with slavery is recognized in the 1926 Convention, which contains a call for 'measures to prevent compulsory or forced labour from developing into conditions analogous to slavery', but this clause is greatly undermined by 'transitory provisions' giving 'competent central authorities' considerable leeway. A similarly qualified approach is evident in both the 1930 and 1957 Forced Labour Conventions, where the primary focus is on codifying the terms on which forced labour can be practiced, rather than on seeking its complete and immediate abolition (Miers, 2003, pp. 134-151, 331-332). Forced labour was a common feature of colonial rule in the first half of the twentieth century. The 1930 and (to a lesser extent) 1957 Conventions would be compromised by efforts to accommodate many highly dubious forms of state sanctioned forced labour.

Another related theme concerns the increasingly topical issue of human trafficking. Until relatively recently, organized anti-slavery and human trafficking campaigns predominantly moved along parallel, rather than overlapping paths (Quirk, 2007). The key historical progenitor of modern conceptions of trafficking is not chattel slavery, but late nineteenth century campaigns against prostitution and sexual servitude. This is not to say that there were no connections or associations, but trafficking – or 'white slavery' as it was then known – would be chiefly defined by a political platform that gave limited consideration to either chattel slavery or other practices of a non-sexual nature. This platform would translate into a series of largely ineffectual international agreements (1904, 1910, 1921, 1933), which were eventually supplanted by the 1949 Convention for the Suppression of the Traffic in Persons and of the Exploitation of the Prostitution of Others. Building upon earlier precedents, parties to the Convention:

> agree to punish any person who, to gratify the passions of another: (1) Procures, entices or leads away, for purposes of prostitution, another person, even with the consent of that person; (2) Exploits the prostitution of another person, even with the consent of that person.

The focus here is not trafficking, which is not defined, but prostitution and pimping.

Over the last half-century the issues associated with human trafficking have been raised in many international agreements, including the 1956 Slavery Convention, but an overarching definition was only enshrined in international law relatively recently. This occurred through the United Nations Protocol to Prevent, Suppress and Punish Trafficking in Persons, Especially Women and Children (one of several supplements to the 2000 Convention Against Transnational Organized Crime), which holds that:

> "Trafficking in persons" shall mean the recruitment, transportation, transfer, harbouring or receipt of persons, by means of the threat or use of force or other forms of coercion, of abduction, of fraud, of deception, of the abuse of power or of a position of vulnerability or of the giving or receiving of payments or benefits to achieve the consent of a person having control over another person,

> for the purpose of exploitation. Exploitation shall include,
> at a minimum, the exploitation of the prostitution of
> others or other forms of sexual exploitation, forced
> labour or services, slavery or practices similar to slavery,
> servitude or the removal of organs.

This expansive formula goes beyond the issue of prostitution to formally incorporate most forms of contemporary slavery. This is in turn emblematic of larger trends. While trafficking and sexual servitude remain closely linked (Gallagher, 2001, pp. 975-1004), many practices have recently come to be analyzed using a trafficking framework.

The final theme to be discussed is the severe exploitation of children. *Child labor* Like human trafficking, the issues associated with child labour have been touched upon in many international agreements. A key starting point here is the 1989 Convention on the Rights of the Child, which contains extensive provisions on many issues, including a call for protection against 'economic exploitation and from performing any work that is likely to be hazardous or to interfere with the child's education, or to be harmful to the child's health or physical, mental, spiritual, moral or social development'. This call has recently been greatly enhanced by the 1999 Convention Concerning the Prohibition and Immediate Action for the Elimination of the Worst Forms of Child Labour. These 'worst forms of child labour' are defined as:

> **(a)** all forms of slavery or practices similar to slavery, such
> as the sale and trafficking of children, debt bondage and
> serfdom and forced or compulsory labour, including
> forced or compulsory recruitment of children for use in
> armed conflict;
> **(b)** the use, procuring or offering of a child for
> prostitution, for the production of pornography or for
> pornographic performances;
> **(c)** the use, procuring or offering of a child for illicit
> activities, in particular for the production and trafficking
> of drugs as defined in the relevant international treaties;
> **(d)** work which, by its nature or the circumstances in
> which it is carried out, is likely to harm the health, safety
> or morals of children.

The International Labour Organization conference which negotiated this Convention also developed a parallel series of policy recommendations, covering a range of issues such as identification, hazardous work, information sharing, and criminalization.

The various instruments and definitions outlined above offer a series of starting points for analyzing and codifying many contemporary problems. It is also important to emphasize, however, that their overall efficacy remains hamstrung by two recurrent problems. The first problem revolves around consistency. Many treatments of contemporary slavery do not reliably adhere to a common set of definitions, resulting in a landscape which is populated by a wide range of often inconsistent models. These variations have also been exacerbated by a widespread tendency to describe particular practices as 'slavery', yet not say how this status was determined. The second problem is concerned with differentiation, where it can often be difficult to determine the point at which slavery begins and other forms of exploitation end. This problem is especially acute when it comes to the approach favoured by the UN Working Group, where slavery has arguably come to be little more than short-hand for virtually any form of severe ill-treatment and exploitation. This situation also reflects an indefinite amalgam of literal (actual slavery) and rhetorical (a loose metaphorical association) claims. Throughout history, slavery has been regularly invoked as a rhetorical device. Familiar examples of this strategy include the concepts of 'wage slavery' and 'sex slavery' used by nineteenth century labour groups and suffragettes. When slavery was legal, the distinction between literal and rhetorical was relatively clear cut, but it has become increasingly ambiguous in recent times. Once slavery is held to come in any number of different forms, it is not always easy to say where slavery begins and ends.

Historical and contemporary models of slavery invariably point in somewhat different directions. From an historical perspective, the main challenge involved in defining slavery is distinguishing between slavery and related forms of bondage, but this approach offers limited guidance in many situations where slavery has been legally prohibited. If we extend the sociological approach favoured by some historians, there are few examples of modern bondage which formally amount to slavery. From a contemporary perspective, the main challenge in defining slavery is identifying which practices and institutions are sufficiently similar to legal slavery that they deserve to be placed on the same footing. This has resulted in a gradual redefinition of slavery, in which slavery is now widely held to come in a variety of forms, which are formally accorded equal importance. In this context, the concept of 'contemporary' slavery, or similar variants such as 'new' or 'modern' slavery, can be viewed as an attempt to distinguish current problems from historical slavery, while harnessing the evocative imagery of slavery to prioritize cases of acute exploitation and abuse. If we were to extend this distinctively modern approach backwards in time, it would quickly become necessary to reclassify many common historical practices as a species of slavery.

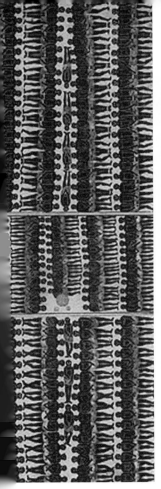

Chapter Two: The Question of Numbers

Slavery has never been an easy subject to quantify. This reflects both interpretive and methodological challenges. Whenever human experiences are translated into numerical values, it is essential to keep in mind the many individual histories that these values collectively represent. On this front, quantitative analysis is best viewed as a valuable supplement to, rather than a substitute for, other approaches to the study of slavery. From a methodological standpoint, the main points at issue have been accuracy and reliability. In the case of Transatlantic slavery, economic historians have accumulated a range of detailed quantitative data, but this level of detail is rarely available when it comes to other historical slave systems, often making it necessary to draw upon a combination of anecdotal sources and informed extrapolations. Similar challenges are also evident when it comes to contemporary issues, owing to both the illicit character of most of the practices at hand, and the inherent difficulties involved in tracing changes over time. In this uncertain environment, many figures need to be approached with extreme caution.

Transatlantic Slavery

These vagaries are less of a concern when it comes to Transatlantic slavery, since extensive data on many issues is now widely available. An important starting point here is the composition of the Transatlantic slave trade. Discussion of this topic usually begins with a 1969 survey by Phillip Curtin. Challenging a series of much higher estimates, Curtin calculated that just under 11 million slaves embarked from Africa, with 9,566,000 surviving the journey (Curtin, 1969, pp. 3-14, 86-93). This conclusion aroused considerable interest amongst other scholars, who have both refined and further supplemented Curtin's initial survey (Eltis and Richardson, 1997). The most comprehensive source of information now available is the Transatlantic slave trade database. When the database was first published in 1999 (based upon 27,233 voyages), the overall size of exports from Africa was estimated at around 11.8 million slaves (Eltis et al., 1999, p. 5). A new version of the database was recently made available online at http://www.slavevoyages. org/. This updated edition revises this total upwards to around 12.5 million slaves, based primarily upon additional information on the Portuguese/ Brazilian slave trade. With the vast majority of slave voyages (nearly 35,000) now incorporated, this conclusion rests upon an impressive foundation (see also Eltis and Richardson, 2008).

These figures are mostly concerned with slaves embarked from Africa. With shipboard mortality averaging around 12.4 per cent (1590-1867), it is generally agreed that upwards of 1.5 million slaves perished on route to the Americas (Klein, 1999, p. 139, see also Klein et al., 2001). It is also equally important to emphasize that these figures do not include people killed during slave raids, or further deaths during transit overland within Africa, which are much less amenable to quantification. There is not only less information available, but it can also be difficult to disentangle slaves bound for the Transatlantic slave trade from those implicated in parallel intra-African and trans-Saharan slave trades. One attempt to come to terms with these issues comes from Paul Lovejoy. According to Lovejoy, over 7.4 million slaves were exported across the Atlantic from 1600 to 1800 (with another 2.3 million being transported across the Sahara, Red Sea and Indian Ocean during the same period). Estimating losses from deaths in Africa at 6-10 per cent at port of departure and a further 10-14 per cent during travel to the coast, Lovejoy concludes that 'the volume of the trade was about 20 per cent higher than the export figures alone – that is, 9.8 million slaves for the Transatlantic trade and its supply network' (Lovejoy, 2000, p. 63; see also Miller, 1988, pp. 381-382, 437-442). This calculation may be fairly conservative – mortality on some routes may have been much higher – but it nonetheless provides an important insight into the dimensions of the intra-African component of the trade.

The Portuguese began trading in slaves on the West African coast in the mid-fifteenth century, and remained Europe's pre-eminent slave traders through the sixteenth and early seventeenth century, supplying both their own colonies and those of Spanish conquistadors. By the beginning of the eighteenth century the British, French and Dutch had also acquired American colonies and established themselves as major slave traders. Over time, parallel increases in both national involvement and plantation production massively increased demand for African slaves. According to Curtin, around '60 per cent of all slaves delivered to the New World were transported during the century 1721-1820', and around '80 per cent of the total were landed during the century and a half, 1701-1850' (Curtin, 1969, p. 265). British traders were Europe's leading slavers throughout the eighteenth century, but the initiative again passed to the Portuguese following the closure of the British trade in 1808. Over the course of more than three and a half centuries, Portuguese/Brazilian traders transported an estimated 5,848,265 slaves, with the British contribution coming in at 3,259,440 slaves, the French at 1,381,404 slaves, the Spanish/Uruguayan trade at 1,061,524 slaves, and the Dutch at 554,336. The United States and Danish/Baltic trades totalled 305,326 and 111,041 slaves respectively (http://www.slavevoyages.org/, accessed 21 August 2008).

The geographic sources of slaves from within Africa would also vary considerably. European traders would do business with many peoples along the west coast of Africa, developing networks which spanned from Senegambia to western central Africa (what is now Gabon, Democratic Republic of the Congo, and Angola). A smaller yet still substantial trade to Brazil was also conducted in southeastern Africa (what is now Mozambique). Different carriers would concentrate their energies on different regions, whose level of involvement in the trade evolved over the centuries. The Portuguese were particularly dominant in west central Africa, which supplied significantly more slaves than any other region (5,694,574). Much of this trade was organized from Brazil, rather than Portugal. The English and Dutch eventually secured a dominant position on the Gold Coast (what is now Ghana), another key source of slaves (1,209,321). Between these two regions were the Bights of Benin (1,999,060) and Biafra (1,594,560), where the growth of slave trading also overlapped with the growth of a number of powerful African states. A similarly variegated picture also emerges when we examine where slaves arrived in the Americas. By far the single largest recipient of slaves was Brazil, which saw 5,532,118 slaves embarked at various ports. Other key regions for imports were Cuba at 889,990, Jamaica at 1,212,351 and Saint Domingue at 911,142 (see http://www.slavevoyages.org/). Further recipients included the Spanish mainland, Guiana, other Caribbean islands such as Trinidad and Barbados, and the north American mainland (see also Klein, 1999, pp. 47-73, 161-182).

It is difficult to overstate the contribution of African slaves to the colonization of the Americas. For European settlements to flourish (beyond initial gains from plundering indigenous peoples), they needed to develop market orientated goods (Fogel, 1989, pp. 21-29). The main avenues were mining, agriculture, and hunting/rearing animals. Of particular importance here was the growth of sugar plantations, which served as the main catalyst for rising demand for slaves from the mid-seventeenth century onwards. Sugar has been characterized as the 'greatest of the slave crops'. It has been calculated that '[b]etween 60 and 70 per cent of all the Africans who survived the Atlantic voyages ended up in one or another of Europe's sugar colonies' (Fogel and Engerman, 1974, p. 16). If African labour is removed from this economic equation, it is difficult to imagine how many European colonies could have prospered (Solow, 1993). One synopsis of this dynamic is provided by David Davis, who observes that:

> By 1820 nearly 8.7 million slaves had departed from Africa to the New World, as opposed to only 2.6 million whites, many of them convicts and indentured servants, who had left Europe. Thus by 1820 African slaves constituted almost 77 percent of the enormous population that had sailed toward the Americas, and from 1760 to 1820 this emigrating flow included 5.6 African slaves for every European … In other words, there can be no doubt that black slave labor was essential in creating and developing the "original" New World that began by the 1840s to attract so many millions of European immigrants (Davis 2006, p. 80).

This overwhelming economic reliance on slavery in many parts of the Americas is relatively unusual. While most historical societies contained at least some slaves, there are comparatively few examples of societies where slavery exercised such a fundamental socioeconomic role (see Finley, 1980; Turley, 2000, pp. 62-100).

Slave populations in the Americas were rarely self-sustaining, and required a constant supply of new slaves from Africa to compensate for low birth rates, unfavourable sex ratios, tenuous relationships, and high mortality. Many slaves would not survive more than a few years in their new environment. The notable exception here was the southern United States. As we have seen, (what would become) the United States played a relatively minor overall role in the Transatlantic trade. In the initial phase of north American settlement, comparatively small numbers of slaves were dispersed across many economic sectors (sugar was never a major force), but their numbers and economic contribution were far less significant than those of their counterparts on plantations in the colonial Caribbean (Fogel, 1989, pp. 29-31). This began to change with the growth of tobacco plantations in the Chesapeake from the late seventeenth century onwards (Berlin, 1998, pp. 107-141). Over time, plantations steadily expanded across much of the United States, buoyed by a population of slaves born in America.

This trajectory would accelerate during the nineteenth century, driven by an almost exponential increase in cotton production. This tremendous expansion was facilitated by a remarkable increase in the American-born slave population, which surged from 1.5 million in 1820 to nearly 4 million by 1860. With US nationals prohibited from the Transatlantic slave trade from 1808 onwards, an immense internal slave trade developed, with close to a million slaves being transported from the Chesapeake and other Atlantic coastal regions to the 'Old Southwest', which centred on the lower Mississippi Valley (Davis, 2006, pp. 182-183; see also Deyle, 2006). This had cataclysmic consequences when it came to the separation of families. The rapid growth in slave numbers does not in any way reflect 'benign' treatment – there is no question that slavery in the United States was exceptionally severe – but can instead be primarily traced to economic incentives. In 1860, the monetary value of the slave population may have reached 3.5 billion US dollars (the equivalent of 63.4 billion dollars in 2003). It is clear, moreover, that the 1860 gross national product was only 20 percent above that of the value of slaves. As a share of US gross national product today, the value of the slave population would represent a staggering 9.75 trillion dollars (Davis, 2006, p. 298).

The legal abolition of slavery was often a very expensive proposition. In a number of cases, the end of slavery was bound up in protracted wars, resulting in large-scale losses of blood and treasure. No government compensated former slaves, but many offered their former masters generous compensation for their economic losses. It is clear, moreover, that introducing restrictions on slavery could also mean foregoing future economic opportunities (Eltis, 1987). This was particularly an issue for Britain, the pre-eminent slave power of the eighteenth century. When the British Parliament abolished slavery in a number of jurisdictions in 1833, nearly 800,000 slaves were involved. Slave owners received the generous figure of 20 million pounds compensation, and provisions were made for an extended period of 'apprenticeship', a new category of servitude similar to slavery in many important respects (Drescher, 2002, p. 4). The introduction of apprenticeship was one of a range of measures employed to placate slave owners and their sympathizers. When the French belatedly freed just under 250,000 slaves in 1848, both compensation for masters and legal restrictions on ex-slaves followed (Blackburn, 1988, pp. 496-506; Jennings, 2000, pp. 280-284). In most parts of Latin America, where slaves were not as numerous as in the colonial Caribbean, officials regularly turned to self-purchase schemes and 'free birth' laws, where children born of slaves attained their freedom upon reaching a specified age (Klein, 1986, pp. 250-253). Other slaves would secure their freedom by serving as soldiers during various wars of independence (Blanchard, 2006).

The last bastion of slavery in the Americas was Brazil, where moves to gradually end slavery in 1871 (the slave population was around 1.5 million in 1872), would be followed by a dramatic period of popular mobilization in the 1880s, culminating in immediate, uncompensated abolition in 1888 (Kraay, 2006, p. 148). During this period the existence of slavery would come to be viewed as a national embarrassment, as Brazilians were humiliated by 'references to their country as the last Christian nation that tolerated slavery, on a level with "backward" African and Asiatic slaveholding societies' (Drescher, 1988, p. 23). This comparison not only introduces the sensitive topic of parallel slave systems outside the Americas, it also raises the twin themes of collective honour and 'civilized' status. As we shall see in chapter four, these two themes would be crucial to the abolition of slavery in many corners of the globe.

Other Examples of Legal Slavery

Slavery has always been a global issue. While Transatlantic slavery has long attracted the lion's share of scholarly and popular attention, it is also important to consider the parameters of other concurrent slave systems.

This topic has not received a great deal of attention in many circles, which is somewhat surprising considering the scale of many of the issues involved. Between 1500 and 1900, both slavery and slave trading were significant issues throughout North Africa and the Middle East, Italy, Russia, the Indian subcontinent, East, Southeast and Central Asia, and sub-Saharan Africa. Detailed information on these regions can be difficult to come by, so any calculations need to be treated as informed estimates, rather than concrete realities.

One theme which has attracted considerable attention is the volume of the trans-Saharan slave trade. A key starting point here is the work of Ralph Austen. In a tentative census published in 1989, Austen concluded that around 17 million black slaves crossed the Sahara, the Red Sea and the Indian Ocean. This figure has proved to be controversial. Another attempt to come to terms with this question comes from Paul Lovejoy, who calculates that around 6 million slaves were transported between 650 and 1500, another 3 million between 1500 and 1800, and around 2 million in the nineteenth century, making a total of 11.5 million (Clarence-Smith, 2006, pp. 11-12). The increasing volume of the trans-Saharan trade during the nineteenth century forms part of a larger pattern. At the same time slavery in the Americas was reaching its historical zenith, slave systems within continental Africa were also expanding rapidly. The scale of these concurrent developments is nicely summarized by Patrick Manning, who has calculated that 'the number of Black slaves in the Americas and sub-Saharan Africa rose from about ten million in 1800 to seventeen million in 1850' (Manning, 2007, pp. 26-27).

The rapid growth of slavery within Africa was a product of long- and short-term trends, as centuries of involvement in both regional and trans-continental slave trades were exacerbated by a range of more immediate factors, including cataclysmic wars in parts of Western Africa and Sudan, the suppression of the Transatlantic slave trade, the rise of plantations and other forms of slave production, and the growth of 'legitimate' commerce with European traders (Law, 1995; Lovejoy, 2000, pp. 191-251; Manning, 1990, pp. 136-148). One major focal point here was the East African island of Zanzibar. By the early nineteenth century, Zanzibar's Omani rulers had established a major commercial hub, which claimed jurisdiction over large sections of the neighbouring mainland. Slavery was at the heart of this achievement. Plantations prospered in Zanzibar, the adjacent island of Pemba, and on various coastal sites (Cooper, 1977). Zanzibar's other major source of income came from the slave trade, where peoples enslaved in the interior were taken to the coast and transported by the thousands in dhows to sites in the Middle East. According to R.W. Beachey, the various branches (both overland and maritime) of the East African slave trade amounted to over two million slaves over the course of the nineteenth century (Beachey, 1976, pp. 260-262). This appears to have resulted in depopulation in parts of central and eastern Africa. Not all slaves were moved north. According to Patrick Manning, slaves constituted around 10 percent of the population of the eastern coast of Africa in the nineteenth century. This amounts to nearly 1.5 million slaves (Manning, 1990, p. 81). According to one colonial survey, German East Africa (what is now Tanzania) was home to over 400,000 slaves around the turn of the twentieth century (Deutsch, 2006, pp. 166-167)

Similar themes are also in evidence in other parts of Africa in the nineteenth century. From Senegal and Mauritania in the west, to Niger in the east (what would eventually become French West Africa), there was a series of ruinous holy wars, or *jihads*, which resulted in hundreds of thousands of people being violently enslaved. In many centres, slaves comprised between one third and one half of the total population (Lovejoy, 2004, p. 6). Here, as elsewhere, we see the development of large-scale plantations, but these operations were often geared towards local requirements, rather than overseas trade. According to Martin Klein, there were between 3 and 3.5 million slaves – representing over 30 percent of the total population – within this sparsely populated region at the beginning of the twentieth century. While these numbers would gradually decline under French jurisdiction, 200,000 people are said to have continued to accept some form of slavery at the end of colonial rule in 1960 (Klein, 1998, pp. 194, 252-259). Another major slave centre was the Sokoto Caliphate, which was primarily based in what is now northern Nigeria. The Caliphate, which was founded in 1804, brought together a loose confederation of around 30 emirates. Having secured regional primacy through a series of wars, it was eventually conquered by British invaders between 1897 and 1903. By that time, its slave population is now said to have grown 'in excess of two million and perhaps more than 4.5 million' (Lovejoy, 2005, p. 3).

The history of slavery in Africa also extends to centuries of maritime slave raids by vessels from the Barbary states of northern Africa (extending from Morocco to Libya). These raids primarily concentrated upon coastal areas in Italy, Spain, Portugal and France, but also extended further afield to sites in Britain, Ireland and Iceland, together with regular raids on maritime vessels. Between 1500 and 1800, slave raiding saw between 1 and 1.25 million captives ending up in bondage (Davis, 2004, pp. 3-26). While Europeans expressed outrage at these incursions, they also continued to simultaneously trade for growing numbers of slaves in West Africa. It is clear, moreover, that this was not simply a question of slaves in the Americas. There were also substantial slave populations in places such as Portugal, Venice and Malta (Richardson forthcoming).

Two other major slaving centres during this period were the Muscovy and Ottoman empires. While slaves do not appear to have been a significant portion of the overall population, it is clear that slave trading nonetheless reached substantial levels. The powerful Ottoman empire was not only a significant player in the trans-Saharan, East African, and Barbary Coast slave trades, it was also implicated in slave trading in the Caucuses, Asia Minor and Central Asia. A useful synopsis of this branch of the trade is provided by William Gervase Clarence-Smith, who observes that:

> Lands to the north of the Black sea probably yielded the most slaves to the Ottomans from 1450. A compilation of estimates indicates that Crimean Tartars seized about 1,750,000 Ukrainians, Poles and Russians from 1468 to 1674. Patchy sixteenth- and seventeenth-century Crimean export statistics indicate that around 10,000 slaves a year, including some Circassians, went to the Ottomans, suggesting a total of around 2,500,000 for 1450-1700 (Clarence-Smith 2006, 13).

The citizens of Muscovy not only faced regular slave raids, they also laboured under severe forms of domestic servitude. By 1649 up to three quarters of Muscovy's peasants, or 13 to 14 million people, were serfs whose material lives and human rights were 'barely distinguishable from slaves' (Richardson forthcoming). Perhaps another 1.5 million were formally enslaved, with Russian slaves serving Russian masters.

If we move further east, we also encounter large numbers of slaves in both Central Asia and the Indian subcontinent. In the case of Central Asia, one estimate suggests that the silk road states of Bukhara and Khiva contained 900,000 slaves in the early 1840s (Clarence-Smith, 2006, p. 14). In the case of the subcontinent, another estimate suggests that there were as many as 16 million slaves during the same period. This figure has been calculated to be 20 times the number of slaves freed in British territories by Parliament in 1833, and perhaps four times greater than the overall slave population of the Americas (Temperley, 2000, p. 177). Neither of these estimates is particularly reliable, but both figures at least suggest that slavery was a substantial issue. In the case of the subcontinent, the enslavement of even fairly small percentages of the populace results in very large totals, thanks to the size of the overall population.

Most slaves in India came from within the subcontinent. It is also clear, however, that India formed part of larger trans-continental networks, which included both overland and maritime slave trading (Eaton, 2006, pp. 10-14;

Clarence-Smith, 1989). Indian Ocean slave trading was an extensive, long-standing enterprise. While detailed quantitative information on the contributions of Arab, Indian, Southeast Asian and African traders is not readily available, recent research on European slave trading in the Indian Ocean has shed some light upon aspects of a trans-continental traffic which both pre- and post-dated its Transatlantic counterpart. One set of estimates comes from Richard Allen, who is primarily concerned with slave imports into the Mascarenes (chiefly Mauritius, Réunion). Between 1670 and 1848, somewhere in the order of 386,410 and 388,260 slaves were shipped to mostly French plantations in the Mascarenes, drawing on a network which incorporated Madagascar, Eastern Africa, West Africa, the Indian subcontinent, and Southeast Asia (Allen, 2004, p. 41). During the seventeenth century, a substantial maritime trade was also developed by Dutch merchants, who drew captive labour from three interlocking and overlapping circuits: an East African circuit, a South Asian circuit, and a Southeast Asian circuit. With the passage of time, thousands of slaves were transported to emerging Dutch settlements throughout the region. Once these enclaves were established, annual imports of between 3,200 and 5,600 slaves were required in order to replenish slave numbers. This level of intensity comes close to that of the trans-Saharan trade during the same period (Vink, 2003, pp. 139, 168).

A number of these settlements were based in Southeast Asia, where slavery was also a major issue. Of particular importance here were the incursions of Moro raiders in the southern Philippines, who may have 'yielded a total booty of some two million slaves in the first two centuries of Spanish rule after 1565' (Clarence-Smith, 2006, p. 15). Other examples include the island of Bali, where slave traders were involved in the export of at least 100,000 slaves between 1620 and 1830 (Vink, 2003, p. 144), and South Sulawesi, where another 100,000 slaves were exported between 1660 and 1810 (Clarence-Smith, 2006, p. 15). While figures on other parts of Southeast Asia are not always available, it is clear that slavery remained an issue in some circles well into the twentieth century (Clarence-Smith, 2006, pp. 142-143, 165-167; Lasker, 1950, pp. 15-68).

Many of the slave systems considered above reached their historical zenith at various stages during the nineteenth century. Most of these systems would have expanded further, but for the growing influence of organized anti-slavery. The three major holdouts in the Americas would end up being the United States (1865), Cuba (1886) and Brazil (1888). The other major focal point here was the continent of Africa, where abolition chiefly took place in the late nineteenth and early twentieth century. Under British colonial rule, slavery was formally abolished in places such as the Gold Coast

(1874), Egypt (1895), Sudan (1900), Nigeria (1901), and Sierra Leone (1928), but in most cases slavery and slave-like practices continued long after these dates (Manning, 1990, p. 154). This period also saw slavery formally abolished in other parts of the globe, including places such as Thailand (1905), Nepal (1926) and Iran (1929), which were not directly colonized. By the mid-twentieth century legal slavery was widely thought to be limited to perhaps 500,000 slaves in the Arabian peninsula (Greendige, 1958, p. 45), where two key holdouts were Saudi Arabia (1962) and Oman (1970) (Miers, 2003, pp. 166, 347, 349).

Contemporary Forms of Slavery

There is no question that the legal abolition of slavery contributed to tangible improvements on a number of different fronts (Engerman, 2007, p. 93). It is also clear, however, that severe forms of human bondage have continued to be a pervasive problem. Until relatively recently the true extent of these problems was not widely appreciated, as many audiences have wrongly assumed that slavery is now confined to the past. This complacent stance has been slowly undermined over the last four decades, thanks in large part to the energy of non-governmental organizations. As we saw in the previous chapter, these efforts have been assisted by a larger pattern of convergence, in which a more expansive approach to slavery has merged with growing activism in closely related arenas, such as child labour and sexual servitude.

Attempts to quantify contemporary forms of slavery face a number of methodological challenges. The most obvious issue here is the illegal character of most of the practices involved. While criminal prosecutions and other sources of information can offer some guidance here, only a subset of cases will have found their way into the public domain. In this environment, it is not unusual to find large estimates being extrapolated from small samples. This situation can be further compounded by the conceptual difficulties involved in specifying the point where slavery begins and ends. This recurring problem is particularly significant when it comes to issues such as prostitution, where it can be difficult to draw a clear line amongst various gradations between severe abuses and 'everyday' exploitation. In this environment, researchers routinely focus on the total number of persons involved in particular types of activities, but do not always seek to statistically differentiate between varying degrees of exploitation and abuse.

One prominent attempt to come to terms with these issues comes from Kevin Bales. In his influential work, *Disposable People: New Slavery in the Global Economy*, Bales seeks to place an outer limit upon the expanding parameters of slavery, arguing that '[h]aving just enough money to get by, receiving wages that barely keep you alive, may be called wage slavery, but it is not slavery. Sharecroppers have a hard life, but they are not slaves. Child labor is terrible, but it is not necessarily slavery' (Bales, 1999, p. 5). Rejecting estimates placing the number of slaves as high as 200 million, he introduces the comparatively modest figure of 27 million slaves as a conservative estimate of documented cases of *real* slavery. The majority of these 27 million come from the Indian subcontinent, where between 15 and 20 million slaves are said to be held in bonded labour in India, Pakistan, Bangladesh and Nepal (Bales, 1999, pp. 8-9).

The figure of 27 million slaves has proved controversial in some circles, while being presented as incontrovertible fact in many others. Bales has repeatedly stressed that his conclusion should be viewed as an informed estimate, characterizing his data collection methods as 'the social science equivalent of the vacuum cleaner, sucking up data from every possible source' (Bales, 2005, p. 96). To show how he reached his conclusions, Bales has also published a table that puts forward both high and low estimates on slave numbers in 101 countries. These estimates may not be perfect, but they are by no means implausible. In most countries, slave numbers are measured in tens of thousands, suggesting a modest yet still significant problem (depending on the overall population). Larger figures are offered for Brazil at 100,000-200,000, Myanmar at 50,000-100,000, China at 250,000-300,000, Haiti at 75,000-150,000, Mauritania at 250,000-300,0000, Nepal at 250,000-300,000, and the United States at 100,000-150,000. Both Pakistan and India are measured in millions (Bales, 2005, pp. 183-186). In one recent work, Bales has revised his estimate for Nepal dramatically upwards, suggesting that 'there are around 2.5 million slaves in Nepal today' (Bales, 2007, p. 98).

By assigning a tentative numerical value (1-5) to each country according to estimates of the national intensity of both slavery and trafficking, Bales also goes on to compare the prevalence of slavery with various socio-economic indicators. Using multiple regression analysis, he identifies a series of statistically significant variables that are said to correlate to the prevalence of slavery. These are: i) infant mortality rates (.61); ii) the proportion of the population under the age of 14 (.49); iii) the proportion of the workforce in agriculture (.34); iv) government corruption (.30); and v) levels of threatened or endangered species (.15). These calculations need to be approached with caution, but they nonetheless point in some fascinating directions, as Bales develops the idea of a causal connection between the prevalence of slavery and variations in overall levels of national development (Bales, 2005, pp. 104-107; see also 2007, pp. 217-219).

Another key source of information on the global parameters of contemporary slavery is a recent report on forced labour published by the International Labour Organization. The report defines forced labour in terms of two basic elements: i) work or services that are i) exacted under the menace of a penalty; and ii) undertaken involuntarily. These elements are not limited to violent compulsion, but extend to more subtle forms of coercion. In this formulation, forced labour occupies much the same role as the concept of contemporary forms of slavery, serving as an umbrella term that sits at the heart of a range of serious problems, such as bonded labour and human trafficking. Working on the basis of a strict minimum estimate, the report concludes that at least:

> 12.3 million people are victims of forced labour worldwide. Of these, 9.8 million are exploited by private agents, including more than 2.4 million in forced labour as a result of human trafficking. Another 2.5 million are forced to work by the State or by rebel military groups (ILO, 2005, p. 10).

In the absence of reliable and widely accepted national estimates, the report relies on a statistical method called double sampling, which involves two sets of researchers working independently in order to generate samples of various populations.

This global figure is further dissected in a number of ways. As a percentage of the overall total, only 20 per cent of forced labour is calculated to be extracted by the state or armed forces, with the rest being extracted by private agents (5 per cent could not be clearly identified). Expressed in regional terms, the 12.3 million figure breaks down into 9,490,000 people in Asia and the Pacific, 1,320,000 in Latin America and the Caribbean, 660,000 in sub-Saharan Africa, 360,000 in industrialized countries, 260,000 in the Middle East and North Africa, and 210,000 in transition countries. Framed in terms of regional population size, the three regions with the highest incidence of forced labour are Asia and the Pacific, Latin America and the Caribbean, and sub-Saharan Africa. In each of these regions a substantial majority of cases involve private agents and economic exploitation, with commercial sexual exploitation accounting for a modest portion of cases (8-10 per cent). A somewhat different pattern emerges in both transition and industrialized countries, where commercial sexual exploitation is more prominent (around 46 per cent and 55 per cent) (ILO, 2005, pp. 12-14).

The report also offers specific information on human trafficking, calculating that the minimum number of persons trapped in forced labour at a given moment as a result of trafficking is 2.45 million, or around 20 per cent of the overall total. In this context:

> most people are trafficked into forced labour for commercial sexual exploitation (43 per cent) but many are also trafficked for economic exploitation (32 per cent). The remainder are trafficked for mixed or undetermined reasons (25 per cent).

These ratios do not take into account significant geographical differences. It is clear, for instance, that trafficking for economic exploitation is less prevalent in industrial countries than in other regions. While human trafficking continues to receive the lion's share of popular and political interest, these findings ultimately suggest that 'the large majority of forced labour globally is not linked to trafficking' (ILO, 2005, p. 14).

The two contributions outlined above are widely recognized as major starting points for information on contemporary slavery. It is also important to emphasize, however, that a substantial portion of research on contemporary problems tends to be structured around closely related subject headings, such as trafficking, child labour, or the exploitation of migrants. These projects are not always explicitly organized in terms of an anti-slavery perspective, but they nonetheless touch upon many of the same issues, activities and agendas. In this context, it is worthwhile briefly examining a number of additional sources of information on various global problems.

Of particular importance is the most recent Trafficking in Persons Report (2008). Produced by the US Department of State, this report offers a comprehensive global survey of recent developments in the field. By defining trafficking in expansive terms, the report is able to incorporate virtually every serious problem which falls under the rubric of contemporary forms of slavery. One important feature of these annual reports is their capacity to track changes in official responses, as countries are assigned a rating based on their recent trafficking record. These ratings can sometimes be compromised by political considerations, but they nonetheless offer a rough guide to changes over time. Another measure that is collated annually concerns data on trafficking prosecutions, which saw 5,682 prosecutions and 3,427 global convictions in 2007 (compared with 7,992 and 2,815 in 2003). Of this total, 490 prosecutions and 326 convictions were for labour trafficking (Department of State, 2008, p. 37). This unimpressive figure is dwarfed by an earlier (and now controversial) 2006 estimate of 800,000 people being trafficked annually across national borders, with millions more being transferred within borders (Department of State, 2008, p. 7).

This is one of numerous global and regional estimates to emerge in recent times (UNESCO, 2008a). In many cases it is not at all clear what methodology has been used to arrive at specific conclusions, yet figures are regularly presented as if they were incontrovertible fact. In a recent article in the Washington Post, a prominent government estimate of the number of human trafficking victims in the United States was revealed to be 'an unscientific estimate by a CIA analyst who relied mainly on clippings from foreign newspapers' (Markon, 2007). A more recent estimate speaks of between 14,500 and 17,500 annual victims of trafficking, rather than the earlier CIA figure of 50,000, but even this lower figure appears fairly speculative. When several case-specific estimates of the scale of sex trafficking were recently subjected to rigorous methodological scrutiny, they were found to have greatly overstated the scale of the problems involved (Gould, 2008; Steinfatt et al., 2002).

Another important source of data is a 2002 report on child labour published by the International Labour Organization. One of a series of global snapshots, the report calculates that around 211 million children aged 5 to 14 were engaged in economic activity at the turn of the twenty-first century. From this starting point, the number of working children is further divided into more narrowly defined categories, with around 171 million children aged 5-17 said to be working in hazardous situations or conditions, and a minimum of 8.4 million children said to be subjected to the worst forms of child labour (as defined under the 1999 Convention). This 8.4 million figure combines human trafficking (1.2 million), forced and bonded labour (5.7 million), armed conflict (300,000), prostitution and pornography (1.8 million) and illicit activities (600,000). The geographic region with the largest incidence of the worst forms of child labour is once again Asia and the Pacific, with forced and bonded labour comprising the bulk of the regional total (ILO, 2002, pp. 14, 23-27). More recent reports point to a modest decline in overall numbers of working children (ILO, 2006), but do not attempt to track changes in the prevalence of the worst forms of labour.

The final source of information that needs to be considered here are the Human Development Reports produced by the United Nations Development Programme (UNDP). These reports are not directly concerned with slavery, but instead provide a snapshot of some of the main structural causes behind many contemporary manifestations of systematic exploitation and abuse. Since 1990, the UNDP has been producing extensive tables of country- and case-specific information. Only a brief global snapshot can be offered here.

One obvious starting point is the overall number of people said to be living on less than 1 US dollar a day, which is calculated at just over a billion people (an improvement upon past estimates), with 2.6 billion, or 40 per cent of the world's population, living on less than US$2 a day (UNDP, 2008, p. 25). Poverty has long been identified as a critical factor when it comes to contemporary slavery, since a lack of resources can not only force people into situations where they become vulnerable to enslavement, but can also contribute to enslaved persons staying in otherwise excruciating circumstances due to a lack of viable alternatives

Two other essential themes are inequality and education. When it comes to global inequality, the poorest 20 per cent of the world's people are said to account for 1.5 per cent of world income, with the poorest 40 per cent (the $2 a day poverty threshold) accounting for 5 per cent of world income. This shameful imbalance can be found both within and between individual states, and has far-reaching implications for migration patterns, social aspirations, sexual behaviour and labour relations. When it comes to education, around 100 million adults are estimated to be illiterate, with women comprising around two thirds of the overall total (UNDP, 2006, pp. 268-269). Despite improvements in a number of areas, recent research suggests that around 75 million children remain out of school (UNESCO, 2008b, p. 61). These sorts of educational shortcomings have long-term ramifications, since the 'large educational inequalities of today are the income and health inequalities of tomorrow' (UNDP, 2006, p. 269). While these structural dynamics are by no means the only factors that contribute to modern slavery – historical legacies, political organization, and social discrimination are also vital here – there is no doubt that they constitute some of the key ingredients involved.

Chapter Three:
Human Bondage in a
Comparative Perspective

This chapter offers a snapshot of some of the main similarities and differences between past and present practices. This is not an easy exercise, since both historical and contemporary slavery cover a variety of practices and procedures. What is clear, however, is that profound changes have occurred over the past two and a half centuries. While some age-old problems remain significant issues in some regions, their overall prevalence has greatly declined with the passage of time. Practices which were once ubiquitous, such as slave raiding, have now become exceptional issues, while new technologies and commercial interests have contributed to enduring forms of bondage migrating into novel settings. Alongside these differences we also encounter underlying similarities, as both historical and contemporary practices share a common core of violence, exploitation, dominion and resistance. In this context, it can be useful to think of an essential core which is then surrounded by many different permutations.

Demand, Acquisition and Control

Most accounts of the historical origins of slavery begin with the enslavement of captives taken in violent conflict. This has often been expressed in the language of a bargain, with prisoners 'consenting' to serve as slaves to avoid certain death. While this formula is not without merit, it only captures part of the issues involved here. It is clear, for instance, that this one-sided bargain usually involved individuals deemed to be of potential value (and manageable risk), with more troublesome adult men regularly being slain. In a significant number of cases, enslavement was not simply an indirect consequence of warfare directed towards other ends, but was also a major source of martial motivation, as internal and/or external demands for new slaves regularly proved to be an important catalyst for large-scale organized violence. One prominent example of this dynamic is the 1821 invasion of Sudan by the Khedive of Egypt, Muhammad Ali, which was chiefly motivated by a desire for fresh slaves and additional resources to help develop his expanding army (Sikainga, 1996, pp. 11-35).

This nexus between acquisition and demand has far-reaching ramifications. Throughout history, slaves have been acquired to advance various interests and agendas. These agendas have played key roles in determining both the parameters of further enslavement and the value of existing slave populations. In most cases this would be primarily an economic issue, with slave labourers being placed in service of various commercial interests, but demand for slaves could also be driven by social, sexual and military agendas. Framed in these terms, the origins of slavery do not begin with enslavement, or with slave raiders and traders, but can instead be at least partially traced to demands generated from within larger political and economic communities, which can therefore bear a degree of responsibility for acts of violence perpetrated on their behalf. This is also relevant when it comes to evaluating differences between past and present. One of the key changes that has occurred in the last two and half centuries concerns the complex relationship between warfare and slavery. While enslavement though violent conflict remains a prominent issue in places such as Uganda and Sudan (Human Rights Watch, 2003; Department of State, 2002), it is no longer routine practice to kill adult males and sell captive women and children into legal slavery. This not only marks a significant change in modes of acquisition, it also involves a substantial decline in demand for additional slaves as a catalyst for violent conflict.

This changing relationship forms part of a larger transformation. Over the last two centuries, there has been a dramatic decline in the number of slaves acquired through violent conflicts, through accident of birth, and through judicial sanctions and tributary obligations. Of particular importance here is enslavement through birth. In a majority of slaveholding societies, birth 'during *most* periods was the source of *most* slaves' (Patterson, 1982, p. 132). The most notable exception here is the Colonial Caribbean, where imports regularly overshadowed births. This horrific fate held some attractions for slaveholders, with subservient attitudes being inculcated at an early age, but it could also require a long investment before enslaved children were productive. While enslavement through birth remains a problem in some countries, such as India or Mauritania, it is clear that its overall prevalence has greatly diminished. Another key issue here is judicial enslavement, which was particularly prominent in societies which enslaved members of their own communities, rather than external interlopers. In such cases, enslavement typically followed a conviction for serious transgressions. This also no longer occurs outside a handful of residual cases, such as Trokosi "cult" slavery in Ghana.

One prominent mode of acquisition which has survived the test of time, albeit on modified terms, is that of debt. In this environment, debt can be associated with both formal and informal enslavement. In the case of the former, an inability to repay monetary obligations culminates in an official determination that a failed debtor should be formally enslaved as a form of compensation. In the case of the latter, an inability to repay monetary obligations serves as a platform for a range of highly exploitative relationships which effectively amount to slavery in all but name. Formal enslavement through debt can be found in many historical settings, from Ancient Greece to nineteenth century Asia (Clarence-Smith, 2006, pp. 76-78; Finley, 1964; Klein, 2005, pp. 203-211), but now no longer poses a substantial problem. Informal enslavement through debt can also be found in many historical settings, most notably in Latin America and the Indian subcontinent

(Kloosterboer, 1960, p. 98; Kumar, 1993), yet also continues to be a serious modern-day problem, having migrated into a number of different settings.

Contemporary modes of enslavement usually involve a combination of deception, violence, vulnerability and desperation. In most cases, debt and deception are closely connected. This often begins with deceitful labour recruiters holding out the prospect of employment on attractive terms. Faced with few appealing alternatives, vulnerable individuals enter into binding work agreements, incurring significant debts as an advance upon future earnings, or to cover associated travel costs. Once established, these debts serve as instruments of control. When victims discover that their work bears little resemblance to what was promised, they are told that they must continue to serve on terms dictated by their new masters until their debts are repaid. Thanks to exorbitant interest rates, fraudulent accounting and various penalties for poor performance, repayment is designed to be an exceedingly difficult exercise, leaving victims to endure sadistic abuses and severe exploitation for little or no reward. Within this basic framework, a debt can be either an individual or collective responsibility, with the latter involving children being called upon to fulfil obligations incurred by their parents, or whole families labouring to meet debts incurred by the head of the household. Another variation on this theme involves families placing their children in the hands of strangers in return for monetary payments. Tragically, these exchanges can be instrumental in ensuring compliance, as enslaved children can be afraid that their families will have to return their sale price if they fail to perform.

Deception usually goes hand in hand with poverty and desperation. People who end up being enslaved through debt and deception are often well aware of the potential for fraud, yet nonetheless decide to take a chance in response to limited alternatives. In some cases deception is not even necessary, as poverty and desperation can be sufficient in themselves. While millions of people are currently enslaved as bonded labourers on the Indian subcontinent, not all of these individuals have been deceived. For tens of thousands of impoverished and landless families, debt-bondage can constitute the only readily available means of securing a tenuous livelihood. In many respects, this represents a throwback to the historical practice of self-enslavement, which a number of slave systems recognized as a resource of last resort, with desperate and vulnerable individuals entering into slavery to ensure physical survival and social protection.

In this environment, poverty and desperation can also play vital roles in ensuring compliance once enslavement has occurred. When slavery remained legal, public officials could be reliably called upon to uphold the rights of masters over their slaves. Most modern slaveholders do not have this luxury (although corrupt officials can be very useful here), so they seek to achieve a similar degree of control using different means. The key starting point here is physical violence, which forms the core of all forms of slavery. In this context, violence is most commonly associated with 'seasoning' in the early stages of servitude and as a strategic platform for discipline and retribution. Not all violence is calculated, but it can also reflect more sadistic urges. It is clear, moreover, that the prospect of further violence consistently serves as the backdrop for other forms of control. When masters assert that debts must be honoured, they do so with the understanding that retribution will follow if victims fail to deliver.

Violence

Another popular instrument of control is isolation, which often includes physical distance from place of origin, language barriers, exclusion from wider society, confiscation of documents, and the absence of larger support networks. Geographic distance and social marginalization can not only render escape difficult, but can also lead victims to endure their current circumstance, however unpleasant, out of dread of uncertain outcomes upon departure. Moves to isolate victims of slavery are common in many settings, but when it comes to illegal migration further disabilities emerge. Unable to seek lawful employment, migrants gravitate towards informal labour markets, which offer fertile ground for many forms of exploitation, with employers flouting legal standards covering hours, wages and work conditions. Faced with the prospect of arrest and deportation, illegal migrants can be very reluctant to appeal to officials for assistance and support, leaving them especially vulnerable to a range of serious abuses.

Isolation

Employers who make use of informal labour markets can greatly enhance their economic prospects by strategically depressing wage rates and working conditions. Many forms of contemporary slavery take this dynamic to its logical conclusion, by reducing returns to 'workers' to an absolute minimum, while concurrently demanding exceptional levels of exertion under extremely unpleasant and/or unhealthy conditions. Aware that few individuals will voluntarily endure such conditions, slave-holders seek to compensate by resorting to violence and other means of control. This formula is primarily applicable to situations that require strenuous, repetitive labour, where slaves can be forced to work harder, longer and for less than available alternatives. Framed in these terms, the chief economic logic driving most forms of contemporary slavery is a demand for greater profits (or lesser costs) than would be available using other means.

Transit and Transfer

During the long struggle against legal slavery, slave trading was consistently singled out as a unique and exceptional evil. This reputation is entirely justified. Many of the most horrific abuses in the history of slavery are associated with slave trading, including violent capture, the torments of transit, the separation of families, and the humiliation of public sale. Especially egregious here is the 'Middle Passage', which saw millions of slaves transported across the Atlantic ocean under truly inhuman conditions. While individual experiences could vary, the basic template remained relatively similar over the centuries. The passage to the Americas usually began with violent capture or judicial enslavement in Africa, followed by an arduous and degrading journey towards the coast, with many slaves changing hands in rapid succession. Before being purchased by European traders, slaves generally endured a further period of confinement in cramped and primitive quarters. Many slaves had no prior experience with Europeans, and were justifiably apprehensive throughout the process of being taken onto an unfamiliar vessel for unknown purposes. Historical sources report many slaves being terrified of being eaten by their exotic captors (Smallwood, 2006, pp. 33-64; Miller, 1988, pp. 379-408).

The horrors of the Middle Passage are hard to exaggerate. Slave ships were designed to maximize their cargo, forcing bound slaves into extremely cramped berths with limited ventilation, where blood and excrement accumulated over time. Diarrhoea, dysentery and disease were routine occurrences. While female slaves were less likely to be shackled and more likely to be allowed above deck, they were also subject to frequent sexual abuse. Depression and torment led some slaves to attempt suicide. If they refused to eat, the crew forced food down their throats using special devices. Extensive nets were regularly erected to prevent captives from leaping into the sea. Shipboard revolts were a recurring feature of these voyages, but they often took the form of a desperate last stand, rather than a well-founded escape plan. Around one in eight slaves perished from various causes. The Atlantic crossing averaged between one and two months depending on the final destination, but slave ships also regularly spent many months on the West African coast accumulating a full complement of slaves, with those who were purchased early in the voyage being trapped on board the entire time. Those who made it to the Americas faced long-term physical and mental problems (Northrup, 2002, pp. 107-122; Klein, 1999, pp. 130-153; Smallwood, 2006, pp. 65-152; Miller, 1988, pp. 408-437).

The history of slave trading is dominated by similar stories of death, degradation and torment, with slavers regularly forcing their bound captives to endure arduous journeys which would permanently separate them from home and kin, leading to their humiliating public purchase by a series of total strangers. Slaves who were deemed too weak to survive transit were routinely murdered, or simply left to die. Slaves who tried to escape or rebel invariably faced severe punishments. Most traders did not deliberately set out to damage their human cargo, but death and destruction were widely recognized as a cost of doing business. One of the worst examples here is the long-standing and often highly lucrative trade in eunuchs, who would be sold in parts of Africa, the Middle East and Asia, fetching between two and ten times the price of ordinary male slaves. To meet this demand, slavers would arrange to have suitable children castrated under primitive conditions. Aware that only a minority of these children would survive (perhaps one in ten), the traders calculated that their increased asking price was worth causing the deaths of the others (Gordon, 1989, pp. 94-97).

For centuries now, apologists of various stripes have been insisting that particular slave systems should be regarded as 'mild' or 'benign', and thus represent lesser evils or perhaps even positive goods. These types of claims were originally made by pro-slavery voices in Europe and the Americas, but also later appeared in relation to non-European slave systems. Regardless of context, such claims about 'mild' slavery have tended to present a stylized picture of the everyday conditions of established slaves, while saying little about either raiding or trading. When these practices are incorporated into the balance sheet, these claims about 'mild' slave systems are revealed as self-interested attempts to dilute fundamental abuses of human rights.

The physical and psychological torment associated with slave trading could also be further compounded by personal and cultural dislocations on arrival, with slaves being forcibly introduced into an unfamiliar social order on highly unfavourable terms. Separated from their homes and kin, newly acquired slaves would have to reconstruct their social and cultural identities, forging new relationships and communities under very difficult circumstances. This process of adaptation is especially relevant to Transatlantic slavery, which brought together different peoples, languages and heritages. A useful synopsis of this dynamic is provided by David Northrup, who observes that:

> Enslaved Africans brought some occupational skills,
> such as blacksmithing and farming, with them to
> the Americas, just as they brought cultural skills and
> traditions. In the mix of Africans from various places

and African Americans in slave societies in the Americas,
particular languages, religions and folkways did
not long survive unchanged, but influenced speech
patterns, belief systems, and musical, grooming, and
eating patterns in the Americas. Rather than isolated
"survivals" of a particular part of Africa, one sees a
dynamic process of reinventing African cultural norms
and identities (Northrup, 2002, p. 135; see also Hall,
2005; Smallwood, 2006, pp. 182-207).

Unlike many slave systems in other corners of the globe, most European settlements in the Americas favoured high barriers to social integration, elevating race to an inflexible marker of social exclusion (see Cohen and Greene, 1972). In some parts of Africa, the Middle East and Asia, 'fresh' slaves – and their eventual descendants – were instead forcibly assimilated into the culture and customs of their masters' community, being gradually incorporated within, rather than consistently excluded from, the dominant social order (Watson, 1980). In both 'closed' and 'open' variants, slave trading would not only involve severe physical and mental hardships, it would also pave the way for a series of far-reaching cultural and social transformations.

In sharp contrast to slave trading, many manifestations of modern slavery are chiefly defined by what happens *after* a person reaches his or her destination, rather than by a set of distinctive experiences in transit. This is especially relevant when it comes to migration and human trafficking, where the pursuit of a better life can lead migrants down a range of paths of varying degrees of legality. If migrants manage to circumvent restrictive immigration controls, they can end up being viewed as a menace to social order. If they manage to circumvent relevant controls, but end up in servitude, they can instead end up as objects of concern. There is not one path for migrants and one path for victims of human trafficking, but many overlapping paths with many overlapping destinations. Unlike slave trading, those involved frequently migrate voluntarily, albeit on the basis of imperfect or fraudulent information.

On this front, it is necessary to return to the twin themes of deception and desperation. Having been offered what initially appears to be an attractive opportunity, victims of human trafficking regularly take proactive steps to reach their destination, including negotiating relevant immigration controls and/or enduring many hardships on the road, only to find themselves enslaved during the later stages of their journey. In such cases, their eventual masters rarely have to employ violence to ensure compliance in transit: the prospect of future rewards can compel their victims forward. This marks an important departure from the history of slave trading, which usually required extensive controls to prevent escape, revolt or suicide throughout the journey. As a general rule, the role of physical violence increases as people become aware of the nature of their predicament. When trafficking begins with an act of kidnapping or purchase, rather than deception, more overt forms of compliance are also more likely to be involved.

When it comes to the process of transit itself, human trafficking can be difficult to separate from economic migration, people smuggling, and asylum seeking. With many governments having further restricted movements across national borders over the last two decades, different categories of migrants have been increasingly forced into common channels (Koser, 2001, p. 71). In this context, illegal migration can take a range of forms, incorporating both long and dangerous maritime and overland routes, and the shorter expedient of travelling by air. In both cases, migrants regularly transit through a series of countries before reaching their final destination. Once air travel enters the equation, close comparisons with the history of slave trading become unsustainable. With some notable exceptions, innovations in transportation have largely (albeit indirectly) ameliorated many of the worst excesses of the past, paving the way for migratory patterns which generally bear little resemblance to historical slave routes.

Migration has long been a difficult and contentious issue, which goes well beyond the scope of this book. It is worth emphasizing, however, that anti-immigration and border protection measures are not necessarily the same as anti-slavery measures (Doomernick, 2004). Efforts to restrict movement will always be an uphill struggle as long as migration remains an attractive or unavoidable strategy. What government action can do, however, is exacerbate its inherent risks, with barriers against entry funnelling migrants into more hazardous and expensive channels (Andreas, 2001; Koser, 2001). It is also clear, moreover, that victims of human trafficking also migrate legally in large numbers, having secured relevant visas and permissions.

The concept of human trafficking has been chiefly applied to serious abuses associated with migration, but it remains less suited to forms of human bondage where transit and transfer play more limited roles. In a significant number of cases of contemporary slavery, extended travel is simply not a major part of the equation, with slaves instead being chiefly confined to every-day drudgery within a single locality. While some victims of enslavement will be cruelly traded amongst strangers (often by purchasing their debts), many others will end up serving under a single master, or under a series of masters representing a single family or organization.

Slave Roles

Slavery has always been a diverse institution, with slaves being forced into service in many different capacities. The obvious starting point here is the slave plantation, which reached its zenith in the Americas, but in addition to field hands slaves have also been extensively utilized as artisans, bureaucrats, concubines, miners, servants, sailors, soldiers and sacrifices. Not all of these roles have been defined by commercial considerations. While all forms of slavery have economic dimensions, these have regularly taken the form of expenses incurred pursuing other goals, such as prestige, consumption, warfare or reproduction, rather than commercial enrichment.

The slave plantation represents the most prominent example of a larger pattern of using slaves in agricultural production. The most onerous feature of slave plantations in the Americas was the gang labour system, which demanded arduous exertion from dawn to dusk according to relentless production cycles, backed by the 'discipline' of the whip and other cruel punishments. The gang system was chiefly associated with sugar plantations, but also extended to crops such as rice, coffee, cotton and, to a lesser extent, tobacco. Sugar cultivation not only required back-breaking repetitive labour, it also required immediate processing once cut, resulting in a further series of dangerous and demanding tasks. While gangs of slaves were usually divided in terms of capability, with young adult males grouped together, heavy burdens would be placed upon all ages and sexes (Fogel, 1989, pp. 23-29). Another prominent feature of the slave plantation was its distinctive social and ideological order, which saw a minority of extraordinarily privileged Europeans based in the 'Big House', surrounded by large numbers of enslaved servants (see Berlin, 1998, pp. 96-99; Genovese, 1976, pp. 327-365).

Other especially onerous historical roles revolve around mines and galleys, which also saw slaves endure severe hardships, hazardous conditions and high mortality. Mining has always been dangerous and demanding, but slaves have featured in a series of severe examples from Ancient Athens to early modern Brazil (Davis, 2006, pp. 41-42; Lovejoy, 2000, pp. 33-34, 121, 172, 199; Klein, 1999, pp. 35-36). A similar story also applies to chained oarsmen, who endured incredible physical demands under horrific conditions. A useful snapshot of this long-standing practice is provided by Robert Davis, who observes that:

> Galley slavery was extremely widespread in the early
> modern Mediterranean, drawing its victims not only
> from the ranks of the enslaved, but also convicts,

> prisoners-of-war, and not a few paid workers. By the
> mid-sixteenth century, both Christian powers and the
> Turkish Empire were capable of mustering huge fleets ...
> It was a labor force that probably reached its maximum
> around the time of the battle of Lepanto, in 1571,
> when an estimated 80,000 rowers were sent into action
> against each other – most of them slaves (Davis, 2004,
> pp. 74-75).

This would be one of many settings where slaves laboured alongside non-slaves. In most cases the divide was not between slave and free, but between different forms of bondage. As an economic model, free labour is a relatively recent innovation (Steinfield, 1991).

Another key issue here is the widespread use of slave soldiers. Having masters arm their slaves may appear counterintuitive, since there is every reason to expect slaves to turn their weapons on their oppressors, but it nonetheless occurred with remarkable regularity (Brown and Morgan, 2006; Crone, 2003; Eaton and Chatterjee, 2006; Pipes, 1981). Arming slaves could be either a formal military policy or an *ad hoc* strategy in response to trying circumstances, with slaves being pulled away from other duties to serve in amateur militias. In this informal variant, slaves were usually offered inducements in order to serve, and often received their freedom by fighting. Perhaps more significant, however, is the use of professional slave soldiers as a major military force. This practice is commonly associated with the Islamic world, where:

> The importance, scope, and duration of military slavery
> ... have no parallel in human history. From the early
> ninth century CE to the first decades of the nineteenth,
> from Egypt to the edges of Central Asia and India,
> military slavery was often the primary form of military
> organization. Even when military slaves – usually known
> as *ghulāms or mamlūks* – did not constitute the majority
> of the army of a Muslim state, they often formed the
> predominant element (Amitai, 2006, p. 40).

Large-scale military slavery was not a distinctively religious phenomenon, but instead reflected various historical precedents and contingent circumstances. In theory, slave soldiers possessed a number of advantages: i) loyalty to their patron; ii) their comparative insulation from larger networks and obligations within society (most slave soldiers did not inherit their status, but were purchased from distant regions); and iii) high levels of training, centralization and professionalism. A somewhat similar logic would also underpin the concurrent use of slaves as bureaucrats, functionaries and administrative agents in parts of Africa, the Middle East and Asia (Clarence-Smith, 2006, p. 88; Sikainga, 1996, p. 6; Stilwell, 1999). These theories would have mixed consequences in practice. While slaves regularly proved to be effective soldiers and administrators, their loyalties could sometimes waver, with more senior figures successfully taking power away from established rulers on a number of occasions.

The final historical theme to be examined here revolves around the use of slaves in various capacities within private households. In many historical slave systems, large numbers of slaves were engaged as domestic servants, taking on cleaning, cooking and other duties. In a minority of cases, this could result in slaves serving as retainers in close proximity to various elites, and thereby indirectly obtaining a certain level of material comfort. This did not, however, alter their precarious juridical status, which meant that things could quickly and arbitrarily change for the worst (Davis, 2006, p. 37). The main issues at stake here were often patronage and prestige, with slaves forming part of larger displays of conspicuous consumption and material opulence.

This connection with patronage and prestige would also overlap with the widespread use of slaves for sexual and reproductive purposes. Especially salient here is the purchase or capture of female slaves as concubines or wives, which is once again chiefly associated with the Islamic world, with large numbers of enslaved concubines serving as both a marker of social prestige and as a channel for reproduction. In many cases, childbirth resulted in increased status for their mother (Lovejoy, 2000, pp. 6-8; Gordon, 1989, pp. 79-104). While concubinage and polygamy are most prominently associated with extravagant harems, enslaved women were regularly found amongst many segments of society, not only amongst elites. On this front, it is important to emphasize that women constituted a substantial majority of slaves in a number of settings, especially within Africa, and thus regularly endured sexual advances in combination with many other burdens (Sikanga, 1996, pp. 21-24; Robertson and Klein, 1984). It is also clear, moreover, that sex and reproduction were not always positively connected. While sexual abuse has been an enduring feature of the history of slavery, pregnancy and childbirth have not always been welcome developments. In the Americas, white Europeans would regularly face social opprobrium for fathering offspring with their black slaves.

Contemporary forms of slavery cover similarly varied terrain. Probably the most significant difference between past and present is that more recent problems are overwhelmingly defined by commercial considerations, with slaves no longer serving as bureaucrats, eunuchs or sacrifices, and only being associated with military service, reproduction and conspicuous consumption in a fairly small number of cases. While sex remains a key issue, it is now chiefly understood in terms of rape and forced prostitution, instead of social status and reproduction. The other major issue is labour exploitation, which can be found in many different settings. Not all of these activities are closely integrated into global markets, but instead routinely involve the production of goods for local consumption, rather than international trade.

A key starting point here is the Indian subcontinent, which contains the single largest concentration of human bondage in the world today, with most victims being enslaved through debt. The archetypal image of bonded labour throughout the region is that of a downtrodden peasant farmer, whose family has been beholden to a local landowner for generations with no real prospect of release. This form of bondage can still be found in rural areas in some parts of the subcontinent, but it has been gradually supplemented by more recent innovations. While bonded labour continues to be concentrated in agricultural settings, family ties and customary obligations have been increasingly displaced by more limited monetary ties between relative strangers, with intermediaries such as recruiters and overseers often standing between 'worker' and 'employer'. These practices can also be increasingly found in a range of settings:

> [b]eyond the agricultural sector, significant bonded labour incidence has been detected in industries including mining, brick making, fish processing, gem cutting, carpet weaving, and such hazardous industries as tanneries and fireworks production (ILO, 2005, p. 31).

Like their adult counterparts, bonded children continue to be concentrated in agriculture, yet large numbers of enslaved children can also be found in other sectors:

> Industries with significant child bondage include silk, beedi (hand-rolled cigarettes), silver jewellery, synthetic gemstones, leather products (including footwear and sporting goods), handwoven wool carpets, and precious gemstones and diamonds. Services where bonded child labor is prevalent include prostitution, hotel, truck stop and tea shop services, and domestic servitude (Tucker, 1997, p. 573).

A similarly variegated picture can also be found in other regions, with labour abuses extending to most corners of the globe, with examples including cocoa farming in West Africa (Ould et al., 2004), cotton and tobacco farming in Central Asia (Kelly 2005), and ranching and farming in Latin America (Breton, 2003; Sharma, 2006).

Like other regions, the Indian subcontinent has also been implicated in numerous reports concerned with sexual exploitation and forced prostitution (Asian Development Bank, 2003; Sen, 2004). As with most issues associated with sexual activity, this topic has proved to be a lodestone for many different agendas. While there is widespread recognition that sexual servitude is a serious issue, there have also been fundamental disputes regarding its overall dimensions and political ramifications. In recent years, a growing number of critics have charged that anti-trafficking efforts have been characterized by sensationalized moral panics that have provided justification for anti-immigration policies, reactionary models of sexuality, counter-terrorism, and the 'rescue industry' (Berman, 2003; Davidson and Anderson, 2006; Frederick, 2005; Gould, 2008; Kapur, 2005). One of the biggest fault lines here has been the contentious issue of prostitution, which has long been a key bone of contention between those who view all forms of prostitution as an abuse of human rights that should be prohibited, and those who view sex work as a legitimate activity that needs to be regulated to prevent abuses. In this polarized environment, debates over human trafficking and prostitution have consistently received far more effort and energy than other related problems. As we saw in Chapter Two, the recent high profile ILO report on global forced labour concluded that labour exploitation was numerically more significant than prostitution and human trafficking at a global level, yet this conclusion appears to have had little impact upon a political landscape that tends to be dominated by sexual issues.

While commercial sex can undoubtedly involve a range of experiences, incorporating degrees of coercion, consent and compensation, there is also general agreement that cases at the bottom end of the spectrum represent a severe problem, especially when they concern children (Davidson, 2005). These kinds of cases typically involve unusually high levels of coercion and physical abuse, an inability to refuse the demands of high numbers of clients, high exposure to health risks and other hazards, inadequate compensation, and an inability to depart freely. While precise data can be difficult to come by, it is clear that tremendous economic returns regularly follow from these conditions, particularly in wealthy industrialized countries (Belser, 2005, pp. 12-18).

The question of sexual abuse is an important issue in a number of other settings, including residual cases of ritual enslavement for social transgressions in West Africa and India, and servile forms of marriage in a number of regions (Miers, 2003, pp. 434-436). One theme in particular which has attracted considerable public interest is sexual violence as part of armed conflicts. Many issues can be identified here, including the systematic use of rape as a weapon of war, but the main issue from an anti-slavery perspective has been the wartime practice of kidnapping women and children as part of organized raiding parties. This is most prominently associated with decades of conflict in Sudan and Uganda, but has also been reported in other recent conflicts within Africa. In the case of Sudan, persistent raids by government backed militias between the early 1980s and 2001 have been followed by the controversial practice of slave redemption, which started with local communities raising resources to ransom slaves and was later taken up by international groups such as Christian Solidarity International and the American Anti-Slavery Group (Jok, 2001 and 2007). Similar raiding parties have also recently been reported in the ongoing conflict in Darfur (Winter, 2007).

In Sudan, thousands of victims of these raids have been forced into service as cattle-herders, domestic servants, sex slaves and 'wives'. In recent and ongoing conflicts in countries such as Uganda, Sierra Leone, Liberia, Angola, Mozambique and the Democratic Republic of Congo, abducted children have also been forced into service as soldiers, often resulting in horrific abuses being inflicted by children upon members of their communities (Dufka, 2005; Honwana, 2007). Not all children have been acquired through raids, they are also recruited through other means. Like slave soldiers, child soldiers regularly provide loyal service (professionalism can be a different matter) without presenting a direct threat to the rule of their superiors.

Slave Resistance

Slaves should not be regarded as passive victims, but as active agents who have consistently sought to challenge their predicament using many different strategies. These strategies can be dissected in a number of ways. On the one hand, we have overt acts of resistance, such as rebellion, flight and even suicide, which revolve around slaves seeking to escape their slave status entirely. These challenges have often been a double-edged sword, with slaves not only bravely seeking a greater measure of freedom, but also seeking to inflict serious injuries upon their erstwhile masters. On the other hand, we also have more subtle forms of 'day-to-day resistance' (Scott, 1990), which revolve around slaves seeking to advance their fortunes while still enslaved. In this context, slaves can be seen as active – albeit severely disadvantaged – participants in a constant process of negotiation and contestation over their terms of service. This is not an easy issue to address, since there can sometimes be a fine line between resistance and accommodation, but this does not necessarily detract from the larger point that slaves have consistently fostered personal relationships, economic spaces, and cultural, religious and social ties under even the most difficult circumstances. In theory, slaves appear as extensions of their master's will. In practice, they represent individual agents whose actions and outlooks have helped to shape their surrounding environment.

By its very nature, slavery requires an act of violent subjugation. However much slave-owners and their sympathizers have sought to conceal this basic fact behind a façade of benevolent paternalism, physical violence has always been an central feature of master-slave relations. One of the clearest illustrations of this underlying dynamic is the extreme levels of violence insecure masters have consistently inflicted upon slaves seeking to escape their situation through rebellion, retribution and/or flight. To discourage further acts of 'disobedience', public officials regularly legalized (or at least endorsed) public torture and other cruel rituals, severe collective punishments, and large-scale and often indiscriminate massacres. In the face of such terrible punishments, direct attempts to escape enslavement have usually required both exceptional courage and extreme desperation.

The clearest challenge to the authority of the master has come through slave rebellions. While the most successful rebellions, such as the revolt led by Spartacus in 73 BC, or the Zanj rebellion in southern Iraq in 869, have severely tested the prevailing political order, these appear to be the exception rather than the rule. In many settings there have been extended periods where few rebellions took place. This is at least partially a testament to planning and co-ordination issues, with many nascent rebellions struggling to move from conspiracy to collective action. When rebellions have occurred, they have typically been on a more modest scale than those mentioned above, but they could nonetheless have a profound impact upon nervous slave owning classes, forcing considerable energies to be expended policing and punishing rebellious slaves.

With the advent of organized anti-slavery, rebellions also acquired additional political dimensions, forcing the pace of legal abolition in many jurisdictions. A key starting point here is the massive revolt on Saint Domingue/Haiti, which is considered in the following chapter. While the scale and success of this uprising is exceptional, similar events elsewhere also had major consequences. In the British Caribbean, to take another key example, insurrections in Grenada (1795), Barbados (1816), Demerara (1823) and Jamaica (1831) would also help to determine the fortunes of the anti-slavery agenda (Craton, 1982, pp. 161-321; Drescher, 1986, pp. 97-110). Once the foundations of slavery had been called into question, political elites regularly faced the question of how long abolition could be delayed before slaves took matters into their own hands.

Another key challenge to enslavement revolves around flight, which has proved to be a recurrent theme throughout the history of slavery. Like rebellion, escape has frequently been a difficult and dangerous proposition, with slaves often being far from home and having little in the way of support or resources, but even unsuccessful attempts could present a challenge to their masters, forcing major resources to be expended to track down fugitives. By seeking to leave, slaves could also diminish their value, and/or signal their discontent by (sometimes temporarily) absconding (O'Hear, 1997, pp. 6-7). Since many runaway slaves could not return home, they sometimes developed communities beyond their masters' control. These maroon societies were especially prominent in the Americas, where many areas fell outside colonial rule. A useful snapshot of their historical dimensions comes from Richard Price, who observes that,

> For more than four centuries, the communities formed by such runaways dotted the fringes of plantation America, from Brazil to the southeastern United States, from Peru to the American southwest ... these new societies ranged from tiny bands that survived less than a year to powerful states encompassing thousands of members and surviving for generations or even centuries (Price, 1979, p. 1).

In many regions, Europeans periodically found themselves in the paradoxical position of negotiating treaties with settlements populated by escaped slaves. These treaties usually concerned peace, security and the disposition of future runaways, often leaving escapees in the paradoxical position of helping slave-owners. These treaties were often tenuous. Armed conflicts would also occur on a regular basis. Like other runaways, slaves who ended up in maroons often faced the prospect of recapture or retribution, making it difficult to escape their status entirely. While colonial soldiers had some success on this front, they could also struggle in the face of innovative guerrilla tactics.

Flight would also play a key role in the historical trajectory of organized anti-slavery. In some jurisdictions, the abolition of slavery was bound up in armed conflict. These conflicts would offer narrow windows of opportunity for escape, with many slaves displaying considerable courage by absconding from their masters and seeking out new opportunities. In both Cuba and the United States, escaped slaves would make crucial military contributions (Ferrer, 2006; Reidy, 2006). The most prominent example here, however, is arguably the Banamba 'exodus', which occurred in French West Africa during the 1900s. The exodus involved between 800,000 and 900,000 slaves, transforming qualified anti-slavery measures into a social revolution, as slaves bravely left their masters, either individually or in groups, and endured tremendous hardships to return to their place of origin, or establish new communities. French officials would do little to actively assist these slaves, but they also refused to consistently intervene to uphold the rights of their masters (Klein, 1998, pp. 159-177). While the scale of these endeavours should not be overstated (a majority of slaves remained in bondage, with female slaves finding it particularly difficult to escape), they nonetheless presented a major challenge to slave-owners and their sympathizers. A similar dynamic can also be found in other jurisdictions, including nineteenth century Brazil (Davis, 2006, p. 326).

When it comes to day-to-day resistance, a majority of slaves appear to have at least partially reconciled themselves to their predicament, and instead concentrated upon improving their lives *as* slaves. A number of strategies can be briefly highlighted here. One avenue for slaves seeking advancement has long been acquiring more favourable terms of service, and/or making long-term efforts to secure their release. All slave systems have made some provisions for manumission, but the specific terms on which slaves have obtained their freedom have often varied greatly, with most slaves in the Americas facing high barriers to obtaining their freedom. This strategy has always come with a number of hazards, with slave-holders holding out rewards as means of ensuring compliance. It is also clear, however, that slaves have proved adept at outward displays of obedience while finding ways of mitigating some of their burdens.

The most straightforward examples here revolve around stealing, sabotage, shirking and independent accumulation, which could all involve considerable risks, but this dynamic can also be understood in terms of more complex forms of contestation and negotiation. On this front, a useful snapshot is offered by Ira Berlin, who observes that:

> Although the playing field was never level, the master-slave relationship was nevertheless subject to continual negotiation … For while slaveowners held most of the good cards in this meanest of all contests, slaves held cards of their own. And even when their cards were reduced to near worthlessness, slaves still held that last card, which, as their owners well understood, they might play at any time (Berlin, 1998, p. 2).

This lens not only applies to legal slavery, but also extends to post-abolition practices, where many of the tangible advances associated with the legal abolition of slavery were not passively received from above, but instead bravely earned from below.

An important example of this dynamic once again comes from colonial Africa, where slaves consistently played indispensable roles in their own emancipation. While 'the slave trade in Africa was suppressed mainly through the actions of European conquerors, the actual freeing of slaves was primarily an achievement of the slaves themselves' (Manning, 1990, p. 161). One key instrument here was flight, with tens of thousands of slaves in many jurisdictions fleeing beyond their masters' control. While most slaves remained within the social and economic orbit of their masters long after slavery had been ostensibly abolished, the prospect of further departures often created narrow opportunities for slaves to renegotiate established relationships (Manning, 1990, pp. 162-163; Miers and Roberts, 1988, pp. 33-42; Sikainga, 1996, pp. 49-57, 95-121). This typically started with terms of service, with slaves questioning the use of severe punishments and the share of their efforts to which their masters were entitled. Other key issues were greater control over the family unit and increased scope to pursue external interests. The usual outcome was not radical transformation, but modest change, with ex-slaves being gradually incorporated into broader occupational groupings, such as peasants farmers or labourers, and broader social categories, based upon race, class and ethnicity (Scott, 1988). In this environment, resistance to slavery often goes well beyond legal abolition, and instead feeds into far-reaching contests over both post-abolition practices and the enduring legacies of historical slave systems.

In the case of contemporary slavery, our understanding of slave resistance is still at a relatively early stage. While there are numerous anecdotal stories of individuals overcoming tremendous obstacles, there are relatively few in-depth studies which are specifically devoted to resistance. What is clear, however, is that contemporary forms of slavery share many of the same qualities as their historical antecedents. While armed rebellion is no longer a major issue in most jurisdictions, flight continues to be a persistent strategy, with many slaves taking advantage of narrow windows of opportunities to flee from their captors. As in the past, flight remains difficult and dangerous, with slaves with few resources or supporters regularly enduring great hardships and the prospect of severe punishments. With slavery now formally prohibited, one might reasonably assume that escaped slaves would be able to turn to assistance from government agents, but effective support has not always been forthcoming, with corrupt and indifferent officials regularly offering little support, or even returning escapees to their masters. When escaped slaves are taken seriously, which is rare in many jurisdictions, they can sometimes end up testifying against their masters, and/or seeking monetary damages through the courts. Neither of these avenues were available in the past.

At a day-to-day level, we once again encounter complex forms of contestation and negotiation, with slaves seeking to incrementally improve their fortunes under a variety of severe constraints. When it comes to their terms of service, it appears that individual slaves have continued to seek out both avenues for advancement and ways of mitigating their burdens. When it comes to questions of culture and community, the diagnosis is often less encouraging. Unlike most slaves in the past, many victims of contemporary slavery are systematically insulated from larger social networks, making it even more difficult to sustain personal attachments and cultural orientations. When slaves are isolated captives, there is generally very limited scope for communal ties.

In keeping with historical precedent, resistance to enslavement rarely ends with slaves being released from bondage, but can also extend to subsequent efforts to establish new lives and livelihoods, overcome past experiences, and perhaps even challenge other cases of slavery. In most instances, this is chiefly a question of recovery and (occasionally) rehabilitation, as former slaves regularly face profound psychological, social and economic challenges while adjusting to life after slavery. This is a crucial issue, since victims of contemporary slavery can sometimes fall back into bondage in the absence of alternative means of support. For former slaves of the 'wrong' ethnicity, nationality or caste, social discrimination and economic disadvantage can also be a long-term burden. It is also clear, however, that freed slaves have much to offer. On this point, a valuable perspective comes from Kevin Bales, who maintains that release from slavery 'generates stability, reduces crime, builds the economy and creates citizens' regularly producing 'an asset to the local, national and world economies', as freed slaves seek out new options and opportunities (Bales, 2005, pp. 18-19; see also 2007, pp. 61-95). Framed in these terms, resistance can not only assist the fortunes of specific individuals, it can also have much larger beneficial properties.

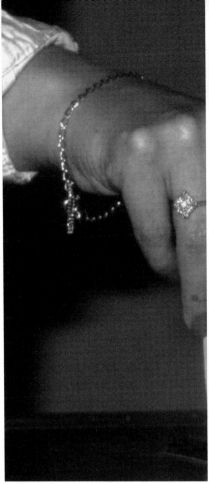
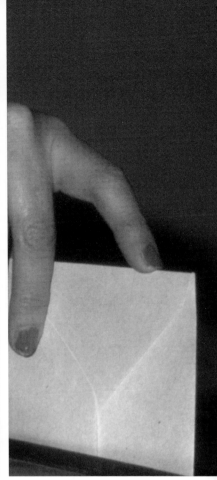

Chapter Four:
Legal Abolition

The legal abolition of slavery constitutes a profound break with thousands of years of historical precedent, with a 'natural', venerable and often highly profitable institution being formally abolished throughout the globe over the course of two and a half centuries. Throughout the history of slavery, there have been consistent objections to the enslavement of the 'wrong' types of people (i.e. untarnished social insiders), but there appear to have been few – if any – *politically significant* challenges to slavery as a *general institution* until the eighteenth century

(Klein, 1993, p. 14; Eltis, 2000, pp. 4-5). The emergence of organized anti-slavery not only required a determination that the end of slavery was morally desirable. All historical societies have recognized that slavery was frequently an exceptionally loathsome institution. It also required a political determination that ending slavery was actually feasible, and not simply a utopian proposition which could be left to moral philosophers and theologians. Until this critical juncture was reached, reformers primarily concentrated their energies upon regulation, mitigation, salvation and/or manumission, rather than general abolition.

The pioneers of organized anti-slavery faced daunting political obstacles, and undoubtedly deserve tremendous respect. It is important, however, not to exclusively concentrate upon political activism in Britain and the United States. These cases are the exception, not the rule. On this essential point, it is possible to identify three main paths to legal abolition. The first path revolves around popular mobilization, with anti-slavery activists building a broad based coalition using petitions, publications, public meetings and other forms of agitation. In this model, which is epitomized by Britain but also imperfectly applies to the northern United States, France and Brazil, a popular commitment to anti-slavery crystallized *prior* to anti-slavery legislation. The second path revolves around violent conflict. In this model, which is epitomized by the southern United States and Haiti but also imperfectly applies to Cuba and parts of Latin America, abolition was bound up in major wars. The third – and most common – path revolves around collective honour, 'civilized' status and external pressures. In this model, which applies to Portugal, Spain, the Ottoman Empire, Thailand and the vast majority of colonial jurisdictions, the passage of anti-slavery laws was not driven by popular agitation, but can instead be chiefly traced to strategic responses and reluctant concessions by political elites to cumulative external influences.

Transatlantic Slavery

The four cases under consideration here are Britain, Haiti, the United States and Portugal. Each country came to abolition via a different route.

Britain

In Britain, as in most jurisdictions, abolition was a two-stage process, starting with injunctions against slave trading and eventually extending to the abolition of slavery itself. This proved to be a protracted process. Led by William Wilberforce and Thomas Clarkson, the British anti-slavery movement endured 20 years of setbacks and false starts before Parliament passed legislation abolishing Transatlantic slave trading in 1807. By the early 1820s, British abolitionists had determined that ending the trade had not caused Caribbean planters to treat slaves better, as they had earlier maintained, and thus initiated a new campaign calling for the gradual abolition of slavery. By this stage, their cause enjoyed broad support within British society, channelling political energies towards the terms and timing of legal abolition, which was eventually passed by the British Parliament in 1833.

The origin and subsequent evolution of British anti-slavery has attracted tremendous interest. A key point of departure here is the work of Eric Williams. In 1944, Williams issued a fundamental challenge to a series of linear histories celebrating the actions of virtuous 'saints' and other political elites, arguing instead that legal abolition was driven by the transition from mercantilism to laissez faire capitalism, with a declining monopoly being destroyed by commercial interests (Williams, 1964; see also Carrington, 2002). This economic determinism would serve as an important starting point for many years, but has now been largely discredited amongst specialists in the field (Eltis, 2001, p. 59). Many substantial problems have been identified here, including inconsistencies in the behaviour of key actors (Anstey, 1968), but the biggest challenge has come from scholars who have argued that British slavery was not a moribund, declining institution, but a dynamic and profitable endeavour with favourable future prospects (Drescher, 1977; Eltis, 1987). By forcibly ending the slave trade when it was at an historical zenith, British economic and political elites appear to have incurred a range of substantial penalties, yet secured no obvious direct material trade-offs.

In this environment, ethical concerns and political activism have made a qualified comeback. One line of inquiry has focused upon the role of popular mobilization, which is said to have transformed anti-slavery from a diffuse sentiment into a viable political proposition. One indication of the degree of support across British society is the scale of anti-slavery petitions. This began in 1787-1788, when a flood of petitions revealed an unprecedented reservoir of anti-slavery support, and culminated in late 1832 with an overwhelming response, with 5000 petitions and just under 1.5 million signatories. One in five males over the age of 15 are said to have participated in this campaign, along with a substantial number of women (Drescher, 1988, pp. 85-94). To explain why this reservoir of support existed in the Atlantic world's most successful slave state, scholars have increasingly focused upon questions of religion, class and nationalism. In this context, ethical and moral concerns do not exist in isolation, but instead gain depth and definition through contingent relationships between slavery, morality, ideology and legitimacy. As 'God's first children', Britons prided themselves upon their unique virtues and institutions. By acting against slavery, they were not so much upholding human equality, as redeeming and/or reinforcing evolving models of their own religious virtue and national exceptionalism (see Anstey, 1975; Brown, 2006; Davis, 1975).

The remarkable achievements of the British anti-slavery movement would have profound international consequences. From 1808 onwards, the British Government advanced a series of policies designed to restrict the slave systems of other states (the activities of British merchants and industrialists are often another story entirely). While the initial target of this campaign would be the Transatlantic slave trade, its geographic and political ambitions would evolve over time. This started with foreign diplomacy, where Britain essentially pressured and/or bribed reluctant elites into legally abolishing/restricting slave trading. By the mid-nineteenth century, Britain had negotiated agreements with rulers in parts of coastal Africa, most of Europe and nearly all of the Americas (Miers, 1975, pp. 40-55). British initiative was hugely important here: '[n]o country in the world in this era signed a treaty containing antislave provisions to which Britain was not also a party' (Eltis, 1987, p. 90). It is also clear, however, that these measures often proved to be ineffective, at least in the short term. Most of the parties involved were not convinced by the anti-slavery argument, and there continued to be considerable economic interests at stake. In a further effort to ensure compliance, the navy was called into action to suppress illicit trading, resulting in an extremely expensive yet only at best partially successful campaign that would ultimately last 150 years (see Kaufmann and Pape, 1999; Miers, 2003, pp. 306-313). At many historical junctures these efforts appeared doomed to failure, but they would eventually undermine both the political legitimacy and the long-term viability of many historical slave systems.

Haiti

Another decisive event in the early history of organized anti-slavery revolves around Haiti, which achieved its independence following over a decade of protracted and ruthless warfare, where 'slaves and free descendants of slaves defeated not only their masters but the most formidable armies of Spain, Britain, and France' (Davis, 2006, p. 159). In the 1780s, this then French territory had rapidly grown to be the most valuable colony in the world, harvesting over half of global coffee production and two fifths of sugar production. With 7,000 plantations, Haiti accounted for 40 per cent of French foreign trade, and had extensive commercial links with other states. This tremendous output was built upon the backs of African slaves, who made up the vast majority of the population: '[w]hile whites and freed coloureds each numbered under 40,000, the slave population, swelling with imported blacks, totalled something like 500,000' (Geggus, 1982, p. 23).

In the wake of the French Revolution in 1789, the population of freed Africans, some of whom were wealthy plantation owners, mounted an increasingly militant campaign for the removal of long-standing racial barriers to social and legal equality. The revolutionary government in France (which previously sought to maintain the *status quo*) finally granted full equality for all free male Africans in 1792, following a massive slave revolt in the north, which could not be suppressed. This revolt became the principle catalyst for a ruthless multi-sided conflict which saw many reversals, changes of allegiance and foreign interventions. To secure the support of slaves against major British and Spanish invasions, hard pressed French commanders issued a general emancipation proclamation in 1793, which was later confirmed by the French National Convention in February 1794. Over a number of years, invading British and Spanish forces were defeated in battle and decimated by disease, paving the way for the rapid ascension of Toussaint Louverture, a remarkably talented black general.

Having repeatedly established his political authority and autonomy on the battlefield (and also reinstituted harsh forms of servitude), Toussaint was eventually seized by the duplicitous leader of a French expeditionary force in 1802, and died as a captive in France a year later. When it became apparent that Napoleon intended to restore slavery in 1802, several key figures who had earlier aligned with this French expedition once again switched sides, provoking a racially dominated conflict which saw armies of former slaves triumph against an all but genocidal campaign by French loyalists. On 1 January 1804, the Republic of Haiti proclaimed its independence, ratifying the greatest self-emancipation in history (see Dubois, 2004; Geggus, 1982 and 2006).

Events in Haiti would have important international ramifications (see Geggus 2001). The impressive exploits of black slave soldiers not only challenged models of racial inferiority, they also offered both an inspiration for other slaves and an object lesson for their increasingly beleaguered masters. From the late eighteenth century onwards, slave-owners in a number of jurisdictions faced two opposing trends. On a political level, slavery was subject to increasing pressure, with Haiti and other similar events heightening concerns about internal revolt, while the cumulative growth of anti-slavery sentiment and legislation resulted in an increasingly hostile international climate. On an economic level, the picture was frequently very different, with slave plantations in Cuba and Brazil going from strength to strength, stimulating an illicit Transatlantic slave trade that lasted until the 1860s, while post-abolition production in Haiti and the British Caribbean faltered in the face of slave competition (see Drescher, 2002). In the southern United States, demand for cotton (mainly from Britain) was the main force behind prodigious outputs and investments.

The United States of America

The legal abolition of slavery in the United States was a protracted, traumatic event. In the eighteenth century there was substantial cross-fertilization between British and American abolitionists, but these links were undercut by the American War of Independence in 1775. Many years later, British groups attempted to support their American counterparts, but their efforts were often counterproductive (see Fladeland, 1972). Across both Britain and the United States, leading abolitionists chiefly drew inspiration from religious doctrine, but the political and legal environment for anti-slavery activism varied greatly between the two countries. In the United States:

> [t]he constitution not only recognized slavery and made it lawful, but also guaranteed that the power of the federal government would be employed to protect the master's right to his human property. Nowhere in the constitution was there a word regarding the rights of slaves or of the duties of masters to treat them humanely. Such matters would continue to be regulated by state and local governments and courts, as they had been in the colonial era, and hence were beyond federal jurisdiction (Fogel, 1989, p. 238)

The procedural obstacles facing legal abolition were further compounded by southern dominance of the federal government, which began at the Philadelphia Convention of 1787 and continued until the mid-nineteenth century.

This reflected both institutional advantages, such as the three fifths clause ensuring that slaves were counted as three fifths of free persons in allocating seats in the House of Representatives, and the long-term support of various northern politicians who consistently sided with the south. Over the last half-century, economic historians have marshalled considerable evidence demonstrating that slavery in the southern United States was not an archaic, inefficient relic that would have organically faded away with the passage of time, but a dynamic and often highly efficient system with favourable long-term economic prospects (see Fogel and Engerman, 1974; Fogel, 1989).

The first phase of anti-slavery activism occurred during the Revolutionary period, where anti-slavery forces had a string of local victories with the legal abolition of slavery in some northern states, such as Connecticut (1784) and New York (1799), where slavery was generally far less prominent than in the south. Many of these measures were geared towards gradual abolition, ensuring pockets of slavery continued well into the nineteenth century (Berlin,1998, pp. 219-255; Zilversmit, 1967). On other fronts, the picture was much less encouraging. While the Revolution raised a series of difficult questions about the status of slavery (during this period slaves represented a little more than one sixth of the national population), the political architecture which eventually emerged would come to be interpreted in a way which severely undermined the anti-slavery cause (Fehrenbacher, 2001, pp. 3-47). In this inhospitable environment, organized anti-slavery faltered for many decades, before once again building support in the 1830s following a 'Second Great Awakening' amongst Evangelical Christians.

It is clear, however, that anti-slavery activists (many of whom were radical pacifists) were only one amongst many forces at work here. In this context, two overlapping themes can be identified. On the one hand, we have socio-economic and ideological cleavages, which saw increasing polarization over many years, with opinion in the north coalescing around the concept of a malevolent southern 'Slave Power' bent upon national dominance, and opinion in the south coalescing around overwrought concerns about anti-slavery conspiracies arising in the north. On the other hand, we have a series of more specific conflicts and compromises, which saw increasingly polarized political and legal contests over issues such as the terms of the westward expansion of slavery, the entry of new states into the Union, and the scope of laws governing slavery in non-slave states. During the 1850s, a fractured electoral landscape would pave the way for the rapid ascension of Abraham Lincoln and the Republican Party in 1860, which in turn proved to be the immediate catalyst for southern secession and civil war. Neither side anticipated the scale of the cataclysmic conflict that followed. Over time, the pragmatic Lincoln gradually expanded his anti-slavery agenda, resulting in a series of revolutionary measures that would have been politically unthinkable only several years earlier. While racism was also pervasive throughout the north, the military advantages of undercutting the southern economy would help to bring popular opinion around to immediate, uncompensated emancipation. This was ratified following northern victory in 1865 (Davis, 2006, pp. 268-322; Fehrenbacher, 2001, pp. 253-338; Richards, 2000).

Portugal

The three cases outlined above have long dominated discussion of the legal abolition of slavery. While there are undoubtedly valid reasons for this analytical focus, it is also necessary to consider parallel developments in other parts of the globe, which frequently occurred through quite different trajectories. One major point of departure here concerns the political dynamics surrounding legal abolition in Portugal. As we saw in Chapter Two, the Portuguese dominated both the early history and final stages of the Transatlantic slave trade, ultimately carrying far more slaves than any other European power. This overall dominance was bound up in two colonial fiefdoms, Angola and Brazil, which were pre-eminent source and destination regions for Transatlantic slavery. In stark contrast to Britain and the United States, Portugal never saw the emergence of a popular anti-slavery movement, and instead primarily came to legal abolition as a cumulative result of external pressures and contingent circumstances.

When the British Parliament abolished national involvement in the Transatlantic slave trade in 1807, the Portuguese were 'profoundly unaware of the issue of abolition' (Marques, 2006, p. 10). This began to change in 1808, at least at a diplomatic level, when the vulnerable Portuguese Government, which was reliant upon British support at many stages over the course of the nineteenth century, reluctantly entered into a series of treaties restricting slave trading (1810, 1815, 1817). Having limited leverage, the Portuguese conceded the right of the British navy to search suspect vessels in 1817, but were able to limit the abolition of slave trading to north of the equator, thereby strategically defending the core of the valuable trade to Brazil. This exception ostensibly closed in 1822, following Brazilian independence (foreign slave trading had been prohibited), which divided responsibility for a then flourishing slave trade into two distinct jurisdictions. In both countries public opinion remained hostile to the heavy handed British, while significant commercial interests in Portugal, Brazil and Angola (where metropolitan control was tenuous) favoured a continuation of slave trading. Frustrated by Portuguese intransigence, the British eventually resorted to the drastic step of unilaterally seizing slave traders operating under Portuguese colours, forcing the justifiably outraged Portuguese into signing a new treaty in 1842. While this treaty gave legal support to the efforts of the British navy to interdict slave traders, it was not in itself sufficient to end illegal slave trading to Brazil, which eventually ended somewhat unexpectedly in the early 1850s, following the use of similarly coercive measures against Brazil (see Bethel, 1970; Marques, 2006; Miers, 1975, pp. 23-30).

It also appears, however, that Portuguese behaviour changed in important ways in the 1840s. This involved a qualified commitment by the Portuguese navy to suppressing illegal slave trading in African coastal waters, which resulted in a much lower incidence of slaving vessels using the Portuguese flag (with other flags now being preferred) and changes in the locations where slavers purchased slaves in Africa. For João Pedro Marques, this transformation can be chiefly traced to questions of honour:

> The big difference in relation to earlier periods was the convergence of national honour and abolitionism … The political elites in government and in the Cortes came to see abolition as an unavoidable necessity, not only for humanitarian reasons or future economic interests, but mainly because Portuguese respectability was at stake (Marques, 2006, p. 181).

In this formulation, it is not necessary to be a committed abolitionist to take up the cause (or, more commonly, signal the appearance of commitment to the cause): challenges to collective honour instead serve as a catalyst for various reforms. This is important on several levels, providing both a key insight into why many states took formal steps against slavery in the absence of popular anti-slavery sentiment, and an equally important insight into why many of these measures proved largely ineffective.

Once the main point at issue is appearance, rather than substance, there will always be many strategies available to uphold collective honour while leaving key features of the *status quo* largely intact. On this front, the Portuguese commitment to anti-slavery proved to be fairly limited. While slavery itself was ostensibly abolished in 1869, a complex mix of legalized forced labour and breaches of relevant regulation ensured that slavery effectively continued long after this date. Despite its best efforts to uphold national honour, Portugal would be vulnerable to British pressure into the twentieth century, paving the way for a series of further scandals and conflicts over disguised slave systems in operation within colonial Africa (Duffy, 1967; Grant, 2005, pp. 109-134).

Other Examples of Legal Slavery

The four cases under consideration here concern India, Nigeria, Ethiopia and Saudi Arabia.

India

The history of legal abolition in India would introduce an important precedent – the 'Indian model' – which was later emulated in many colonial jurisdictions. Indian slavery was characterized by a high degree of variation, with the key social marker being caste-based social hierarchies, rather than race (see Eaton, 2006; Patnaik and Dingwaney, 1985). Instead of being concentrated in market-oriented, capitalist ventures, slaves occupied diverse roles within a complex social order. Since it came under the jurisdiction of the chartered East India Company, slavery in India was not included when the British Parliament formally abolished slavery in 1833. When British abolitionists belatedly took up this omission, many were surprised to learn that slaves in India were far more numerous than in the colonial Caribbean (Temperley, 2000).

With limited resources available to govern vast territories, the East India Company had strong incentives not to antagonize powerful local slave owners. The solution which followed is usefully summarized by Suzanne Miers, who states that:

> Under humanitarian and parliamentary attack, the Company found an ingenious solution – one which was to become the model of the future. It did not outlaw slavery, but simply declared that it had no legal standing in British India. Henceforth, if slaves left their owners, they could not be recovered by legal action or forced, nor could they be made to work … However, it was not illegal to own slaves, and slaves did not have to change their status. Theoretically, therefore, those who remained as slaves did so voluntarily. Thus, the idea of "voluntary" of "permissive" slavery was born (Miers, 2003, pp. 30-31).

This 1843 legislation was publicly presented as a blow against slavery, initially alarming some sections of the Indian population. In practice, it proved impotent in both design and implementation. In 1860/61 the Indian Penal Code introduced stronger provisions, making trading and holding slaves a criminal offence, punishable by up to ten years' incarceration, but this does not appear to have precipitated a decisive break with the past. Most slaves were not made aware of the new provisions. It is clear, moreover, that slavery often had more to do with custom and convention than British legislation (which did not extend to 'Princely States' covering two fifths of the subcontinent). By concealing slavery under various euphemisms, such as 'servants', 'serfs' or 'family members', and/or transferring servile relationships into other legally-sanctioned channels, such as debt-bondage and indentured labour, many masters found various ways of ensuring that the colonial state continued to uphold the tenor of their earlier prerogatives (see Chatterjee, 1999 and 2006; Prakesh, 1990).

In this environment, debt-bondage has frequently been identified as an effective substitute for slavery. This position is captured by M.L. Bush, who observes that:

> Bonded labour thrived in colonial India. For it to do so, only minor shifts and adjustments were required. Thus, with slavery abolished in 1843, ex-slaves were transformed into debt bondsmen. Domestics were now seen as bound to their masters and therefore obliged to serve them. Agricultural workers were now seen as bonded to the land by the debt they had incurred from their masters' generosity (Bush, 2000, p. 216).

This statement is a rough simplification of a complex, variegated process, but it nonetheless encapsulates a neglected transformation. While bonded labour was not in itself a new phenomenon, it would gradually acquire greater prominence in response to various institutional and economic pressures under colonial rule. The non-commercial functions which relatively privileged slaves had historically performed would slowly fade from view, but bonded labour would ultimately retain/secure a substantial economic presence in many sectors. This in turn has major implications for how we approach contemporary problems. As we have seen, the Indian subcontinent is home to the largest concentration of slavery in the world today. This state of affairs can be ultimately traced to a failure to effectively abolish slavery in 1843, pointing to the inherent limitations of the concept of 'new' slavery (Bales, 1999). Instead of reflecting distinctively modern innovations, many serious contemporary problems can be traced to long-term failings which stem from the way in which slavery was legally abolished.

Nigeria

The 'Indian Model' would be used in many territories, offering an inexpensive, non-confrontational approach to legally defining slavery out of existence. While colonial authorities regularly moved against large-scale slave raiding and trading, which were viewed as a threat to order, they were usually far more circumspect where slavery itself was concerned. One illustration of this far-reaching dynamic comes from British rule in Nigeria, where the slave population may have reached several million. Like most colonial inventions, Nigeria brings together an uncomfortable amalgam of cultural and religious groupings. This is a product of piecemeal colonization, as coastal enclaves such as Lagos provided a platform for incursions from the 1850s onwards, culminating in a series of major wars in the northern interior. Here, as elsewhere, we find anti-slavery rhetoric being invoked to justify wars of conquest, but this rhetoric did not translate into a pro-active commitment once colonial authority was established.

This historical trajectory is encapsulated by Paul Lovejoy and Jan Hogendorn:

> By the 1890s, the century-long abolitionist crusade had found its way into imperialist rhetoric … Afterwards, colonial policies attempted to protect local economies, and hence the slave masters, from the inevitable dislocation associated with abolition. Now the anti-slavery movement was radical neither in effect nor in intent: it first served to rationalize imperial ambitions, and then it became a conservative force in protecting the very people who exploited slaves (Lovejoy and Hogendorn, 1993, p. 27)

In this context, the fortunes of individual slaves varied markedly. As in French West Africa, the initial phases of British rule saw hundreds of thousands of slaves leave their masters (Nwokeji, 1998, pp. 331-332; Lovejoy and Hogendorn, 1993, p. 32; Ohadike, 1999, pp. 199-203), but this trend often tapered off once colonial rule was more firmly established. It is clear, however, that the substantial majority of slaves remained with their masters, reflecting long-term socialization, effective surveillance and/or a lack of alternatives. Another key change was the end of large-scale slave raiding and trading. The latter did not cease immediately and instead underwent a slow decline, with some anti-slave trade patrols continuing into the 1930s (Ubah, 1991, pp. 447-470), but without sufficient fresh supplies, slave numbers were not demographically self-sustaining. With the long-term prospects of slavery under threat, masters would face modest incentives to treat slaves better, while restructuring their terms of service. In theory, the legal status of slavery was formally abolished, but native courts and other measures were informally used to police master-slave relationships, with tens of thousands of slaves being forced into forms of self-ransom based upon extended service. Similar measures were also applied in the case of slave concubines, as female slaves were also ransomed to third parties, such as prospective husbands and concerned relatives. Despite the fact that most slaves in Nigeria were women, British authorities regularly collapsed their status into marriage (Lovejoy and Hogendorn, 1993, pp. 98-260; O'Hear, 1997, pp. 62-142).

Decades after British conquest, colonial Nigeria remained an uncomfortable hybrid. Slavery was in decline following flight, redemption, and institutional pressures, yet a substantial minority of slaves remained. Some slaves had secured their freedom, and thereby migrated into new labour systems. Others continued relationships with their masters, seeking out new terms of service with varying degrees of success. In this context, it was not always easy to draw a line between slavery, servitude and freedom. An even greater problem, however, was that few allowances were made for slaves who experienced little change. Nigeria is of particular interest here, since it was one of the few cases where a reasonably detailed survey was conducted, following pressure from the British representative on the League of Nations Advisory Committee of Experts on Slavery (Miers, 2003, pp. 216-232, 278-294). In a survey of the northern provinces in 1935-36, it was calculated that there were 121,005 slaves continuing to live 'in their previous mode.' This figure may have understated the problem (390,000 to 400,000 may be more accurate), but it still proved to be sufficiently embarrassing to provoke a further round of reform in 1936 (Lovejoy and Hogendorn, 1993, pp. 277-284).

Ethiopia

In both of the cases outlined above, legal abolition was bound up in colonial rule. For the dozen or so states in Africa, the Middle East and Asia who were fortunate enough to escape formal colonization, legal abolition would take a somewhat different path. Faced with external pressure to adopt measures against slavery, indigenous elites in these regions initially responded in much the same way as their earlier Portuguese counterparts: delay, deflection and reluctant concessions. While these reactions may be broadly comparable, they often took place in quite different contexts. For most non-European elites, the key issue was not so much slavery *per se*, but instead what slavery was held to signify about the 'backward' character of their communities (Quirk, 2006, p. 588). This would be both a symbolic and substantive issue, with the status of slavery serving as a key litmus test for both collective honour and sovereign recognition.

These themes are particularly evident in the case of Ethiopia. In 1896, Ethiopia inflicted a major defeat upon Italian invaders and thereby cemented its unique status as the only state to escape the European 'scramble' for Africa. Having maintained their political independence by force of arms, Ethiopian elites found themselves in a somewhat precarious position surrounded by Italian, British and French colonies. In this environment, slavery emerged as a key political issue. According to anti-slavery activists, the slave population of Ethiopia was upwards of two million (this probably overstated matters), from an estimated total population of ten million. The incursions of slave raiders, including raids into neighbouring territories, were especially notorious (Simon, 1930, pp. 12, 26, 30-34). To placate critics, Ethiopian rulers repeatedly proclaimed restrictions on slave trading, but official weakness/complicity and domestic opposition ensured that these measures were largely ineffectual (Miers, 2003, pp. 66-86).

Ethiopia was the subject of considerable international debate following the end of the Great War. A key moment came in 1923, when Ethiopia applied for membership to the League of Nations following a sustained period of adverse publicity on slavery (Allain, 2006; Gong, 1984, pp. 124-129). After extended debates in which slavery was a prominent theme, Ethiopia was formally admitted to the League on the condition that it would 'observe the St. Germain Arms Convention of 1919, provide the council with information on slavery, and consider League recommendations on obligations under the covenant' (ladarola, 1975, p. 620). This placed slavery in Ethiopia on the international agenda, leading to extended discussions in a number of forums. In an effort to diffuse external pressures, Ethiopian elites adopted a series of anti-slavery measures designed to demonstrate their good faith, but these once again proved largely ineffectual, as slaving remained both profitable and legitimate (Edwards, 1982; Miers, 2003, pp. 239-253).

This deadlock was ultimately broken by the Italian invasion of 1935. Following historical precedent, the Italian Government turned to anti-slavery to help justify their unprovoked aggression. Here, as elsewhere, the status of slavery was invoked as an symbol of the 'backward' character of Ethiopia as a whole. The Italians publicly maintained that their bloody conquest (which included using chemical weapons) was perfectly legitimate given Ethiopia's 'uncivilized' state, which rendered European 'tutelage' both desirable and necessary. As part of their submission to the League of Nations seeking to justify their conduct, the Italian Government would argue that:

> The survival in Ethiopia of slavery and of the similar
> institution termed gebbar not only constitutes a horrible
> offence against civilisation and an open breach of the
> obligations imposed by article 23 of the Covenant of the
> League of Nations, but also represents a flagrant violation
> of the special obligations assumed by the Ethiopian
> Government at the time of admission to the League
> (League of Nations, 1935, p. 46).

The abolition of slavery would be hailed as one of the 'benefits' of Italian occupation, forcing European critics to confront arguments that they had earlier made in other settings. When Ethiopia regained its independence in the early 1940s as part of British campaigns against Italian possessions, it proved to be politically impossible to retain slavery, and the newly restored Emperor Haile Selassie moved to formally abolish the institution in 1942. This decree marked an important milestone, but it was some years before a degree of effective authority could be restored. Reports of small-scale slaving continued well into the second half of the twentieth century (Derrick, 1975, pp. 150-158; Greenidge, 1958, pp. 45-47).

Saudi Arabia

The final case to be considered here is Saudi Arabia. Viewed from a contemporary perspective, the final stages in the struggle against legal slavery can take on a certain degree of inevitability, creating the impression that any lingering resistance was swept away by an almost inexorable tide. This is somewhat misleading: political elites in the Arabian peninsula generally refused to consider legal abolition until after the Second World War. In earlier periods, there were few indications that they were prepared to prohibit slavery itself, as opposed to restricting international slave trading (which once again occurred through British pressure). The key holdout here was arguably Saudi Arabia, which emerged as both the largest state in the region and the home of the two holiest sites of the Islamic faith. These sites were not only of tremendous symbolic and religious importance, they also served as a long-standing destination for slave traders, with trading in slaves regularly forming part of (or, once the trade was legally abolished, sometimes being concealed under) pilgrimages to Mecca.

Legal abolition in Saudi Arabia would take more than 100 years. In 1855-56, the Ottoman empire was faced with an internal rebellion in parts of what is now Saudi Arabia, where the prospect of the abolition of the slave trade served as a rallying point for armed opposition. While order was eventually restored, the status of slavery remained a sensitive political issue for many years, with authorities making no further attempts to even nominally restrict the trade until the late 1870s (Ochsenwald, 1980). After Ottoman rule collapsed during the Great War, the newly independent state of Hijaz carved out a niche as a major destination point for slave trading. This presented a problem for the British navy, undercutting nineteenth century agreements to legally search suspected slave traders. During the 1920s, Hijaz was one of several regions united under the rule of Ibn Saud, who named his new state Saudi Arabia, but when the Saudis sought assistance from Britain to join the League of the Nations, the status of slavery would play a part in their refusal to offer support (Miers, 2003, pp. 87-99, 254).

Slavery proved to be a recurrent international problem for Saudi Arabia. One important flashpoint was the contentious practice of consular manumission, which saw British consuls in Jeddah exercise an unusual power to release fugitive slaves who sought sanctuary. This intrusive authority was deeply resented (royal slaves were amongst those involved), and formed a key part of combative negotiations in the 1930s, which paved the way for new regulations in 1936 that prohibited imports of slaves by sea, restricted overland imports, provided for slave registration and slave welfare, and allowed for slaves to buy their freedom (Lewis, 1990, pp. 167-169). In return for these regulations, the British formally renounced consular manumission. Like many similar anti-slavery proclamations, these measures appear to have been at best sporadically enforced, with some officials not even being aware of their existence.

Following the end of the Second World War, slavery in Saudi Arabia reached a larger audience through a series of often sensational news reports outlining covert slave trading from parts of Africa and Central Asia. The political dynamics that surrounded slavery are summarized by Murray Gordon, who argues that the existence of slavery:

> made the country and its leaders vulnerable to criticism in the United Nations and among progressive Arab leaders. Slavery was incompatible with rapid economic development and was totally at odds with the image it was trying to project in the Western world. Perpetuation of slavery would almost certainly lead to unpleasant situations with the newly emerging African nations which would regard the enslavement of their people as an affront to their dignity (Gordon, 1989, p.232)

In 1962, the status of slavery was caught up in larger events, with an ailing King being sidelined by his brother during a time of regional turmoil. This new regime proclaimed an end to slavery on 6 November 1962, promising compensation to 'deserving' masters. The impact of this measure is hard to evaluate. While slavery appears to have fallen away, the pace of change is not easy to verify (Clarence-Smith, 2006, pp. 181-184; Gordon, 1989, pp. 225-234; Miers, 2003, pp. 179-183, 254-277, 347-350). Over time, vulnerable migrant workers have emerged as a favoured substitute. In a 2004 report on the widespread abuse of migrant workers, Human Right Watch calculated that around 8.8 million expatriates coexisted alongside an indigenous Saudi population of around 18 million (Brown and Saunders, 2004, p. 8). Some migrants will now be serving under employers who would have previously owned slaves.

The Legal Abolition of Slavery as an Essential First Step, Rather than a Decisive Endpoint

The proceeding analysis is in no way exhaustive, but it does serve to briefly highlight a number of core themes. Firstly, it is important to emphasize that the legal abolition of slavery throughout the globe usually had more to do with questions of collective honour and identity than a principled commitment to human dignity and equality. At both a domestic and an international level, the status of slavery and the slave trade would come to be construed as a key determinant of 'civilized' status and national virtue (or vice), creating moderate incentives for political elites who were not committed to the anti-slavery cause to publically signal their commitment to combating slavery. For these elites, (being seen to be) taking action against slavery represented a symbolic yet nonetheless politically significant test of their 'civilized' credentials and collective honour. Popular mobilization and political activism of the kind commonly associated with William Wilberforce and William Garrison constitutes the historical exception, not the rule. Genuine adherents to the anti-slavery cause have frequently been in short supply, yet the last two and a half centuries have witnessed a remarkable global change, at least at a legislative level.

Secondly, it is important to emphasize that the passage of anti-slavery legislation was not primarily determined by commercial interests. In most jurisdictions, the main economic calculation involved in debates over legal abolition revolved around efforts to *minimize* costs, rather than maximize commercial gains. By legally abolishing slavery, political and economic elites regularly expended substantial amounts of blood and treasure, yet failed to secure equivalent gains. This includes both foregone economic opportunities and the costs of adjusting to alternative labour systems. In the case of the former, there were a number of cases where relevant elites were well placed to expand their involvement in slavery and slave trading, yet failed to take advantage of various opportunities. A good example here is Britain, which was the premier slaver of the Atlantic world in the eighteenth century, but then unilaterally withdrew in 1808 despite being in a prime position for further expansion. In the case of the latter, the main point at issue was the substantial resources and productive potential which had often been invested in slavery over many centuries. For slave-owners, legal abolition usually meant i) the loss of substantial investments/assets, and ii) the additional costs of finding suitable replacements for positions that would otherwise have been occupied by slaves. The legal abolition of slavery would never be a singular, unshakable goal where no effort was spared, but there were also many cases where it would have been far easier to adopt a policy of non-interference, or to take direct advantage of the various commercial opportunities that slavery afforded.

Thirdly, it is important to emphasize the indispensible contribution of slaves and ex-slaves to the anti-slavery cause, both pre- and post-abolition. Many of the substantive advances associated with the legal abolition of slavery were not passively received from above, but instead bravely earned from below, as slaves and ex-slaves consistently took advantage of the narrowest of opportunities to pursue their own vision of freedom. This usually involved i) challenging the authority of their masters through force or arms, ii) forging new lives and livelihoods beyond their masters' control, and iii) renegotiating their terms of service in a variety of ways. These long-term activities regularly placed slaves and ex-slaves in conflict with masters, former masters, and ruling classes. As we shall see in the following chapter, political elites consistently used their privileged position to undermine the interests of slaves and ex-slaves in various ways, resulting in further contests over the nature of anti-slavery, human rights, and minimum standards of dignity and equality. In this context, the legal abolition of slavery is best understood as a qualified first step in a larger and still ongoing struggle to end all forms of exploitation and discrimination.

Finally, it is important to briefly reflect upon the strengths and weaknesses of legal solutions to complex problems. It is now well documented that some issues and activities are more receptive to forms of political activism and argument than others (Keck and Sikkink, 1998, pp. 8-32; Crawford, 2002, pp. 11-130). Because slavery was heavily reliant upon the sanction and support of government officials, historical slave systems remained relatively vulnerable to political challenge on a number of fronts. In the vast majority of cases, opposition to slavery would be channelled into a simple, straightforward solution: legal abolition (of either slave trading or slavery itself). It was not always clear how this solution would be implemented, but there was usually little doubt about what needed to be done. In this environment, the politics of anti-slavery frequently came down to a basic question: was slavery legally sanctioned or legally prohibited? There is no doubt that this line of argument was politically effective, but it would also leave the anti-slavery cause with very little momentum once legal abolition took place. In case after case, governments would disingenuously claim that the legal abolition of slavery marked the end of their anti-slavery obligations, leaving a range of closely-related practices and systemic problems unresolved.

Chapter Five: Effective Emancipation

The recent history of organized anti-slavery has been defined by a somewhat belated recognition of the limitations of the legal abolition of slavery. This recognition has found expression in a broader and deeper understanding of anti-slavery. On the one hand, we have a broadening of the types of practices that fall under the anti-slavery agenda. On the other, we have a deeper diagnosis of the types of measures which are required to address them. This evolving agenda incorporates both modern slavery and historical legacies. In the case of modern slavery, it is now widely accepted that legal injunctions are necessary but not sufficient, and that concerted action is also required when it comes to issues such as prevention, rehabilitation, amelioration and larger socioeconomic reforms. This marks a departure from the 'sink or swim' approach usually associated with legal abolition. In the case of historical legacies, there has been a growing appreciation that patterns of enslavement have often had lasting consequences, and that some form of restitution and recognition is required. While legal abolition continues to be regarded as an important milestone, it is clear that something more is required: effective emancipation (Quirk, 2008).

Effective emancipation is not a static, singular standard, but instead encapsulates an evolving combination of practical politics and ethical ideals. For hundreds of years now, the political horizons of organized anti-slavery have undergone continual reinvention. The pioneers of British anti-slavery initially focused on their own country, but once the slave trade was abolished, their energies also turned to trading by other countries. When slavery itself was later abolished, the fortunes of ex-slaves emerged as an object of concern. These shifts were not only rooted in specific victories, they also reflected a partial recognition of their inherent limitations: if slavery were to expand in other countries, or persist under another name, this would invariably call into question the efficacy of the overall project (Quirk, 2006, p. 586). Recent anti-slavery activism has followed the same underlying logic, with reflections upon the strengths and weaknesses of earlier outcomes serving as a platform for ongoing efforts to further advance the ideal of ending all manifestations of slavery and servitude.

Legal Abolition and its Aftermath

The legal abolition of slavery is often presented as an historical endpoint, leaving the impression that subsequent events marked a decisive break with the earlier *status quo*. This complacent viewpoint conceals a range of complex, uncomfortable and enduring questions. When it comes to post-abolition shortcomings, four overlapping strands can be identified. First, we have the persistence of slavery and slave-like practices in many jurisdictions long after slavery had ostensibly been abolished. As we have seen, the legal abolition of slavery did not always involve a definitive change in status according to a clear timetable, but could also take the form of a 'slow death', which sometimes involved substantial numbers of slaves remaining in place decades later. Second, we have the growth of closely related forms of servitude, most notably forced, bonded and indentured labour, in many quarters following legal abolition. In this strand, the expansion of other abusive labour practices can be traced to strategic responses to the legal abolition of slavery. Third, we have the parallel continuation of related forms of human bondage. This strand brings together practices which share key features in common with historical slave systems, such as serfdom or forced prostitution, but which are not always directly connected to the specific events surrounding legal abolition. The main issue here is similarity, rather than causality. Finally, we have the long-term structural and ideological legacies of historical patterns of enslavement, which can be linked to lasting problems of racism, discrimination and intergenerational deprivation.

When it comes to legal abolition and its aftermath, it is important to emphasize that at no stage during the history of abolition were slaves offered compensation for their horrific experiences, and instead made their way in the world with the resources, skills and patterns of behaviour they accumulated while enslaved. This is captured by Eric Foner, who observes that former slaves received 'Nothing but Freedom' (Foner, 1984). This unfavourable starting point would also be further complicated by former slave-owners and their sympathizers, who consistently sought to retain as many of their earlier prerogatives as possible, and by political authorities concerned about social stability and economic development. In the face of these tremendous obstacles, most former slaves secured a range of qualified yet still consequential improvements in their overall fortunes.

One influential synopsis of these often difficult issues comes from Frederick Cooper:

> Never, as far as is known, has a slave community regretted its freedom; never, even in the face of the most dire poverty, has it wished to return to the security and oppression of slavery. But emancipation – in the southern United States, in the Caribbean, in Brazil, and in parts of Africa as well – has been a time of disillusionment as well as joy. The individual plantation owner may have ceased to be lord and master over his slaves, but the planter class did not lose its power … in case after case, a particular class … kept land from the eager hands of ex-slaves and vigorously applied the instruments of state and the law to block ex-slaves' access to resources and markets, to restrict their ability to move about, bargain or refuse wage labor, and to undermine their attempts to become independent producers (Cooper, 1980, p. 1).

In this challenging environment, freedom would never be a glorious, uninhibited condition, but a subject for long-term personal and political contestation. Of particular importance here are questions of ideology and labour. In the case of ideology, it is important to resist the temptation to project modern notions of human equality backwards through time. Until at least the mid-twentieth century, the social universe was divided into elaborate ideological and institutional hierarchies, which applied both between communities, such as European colonizers and 'native' peoples, and within communities, such as caste distinctions in India or racial cleavages in the United States. The vast majority of former slaves would find themselves in 'inferior' groups, ensuring their freedom was circumscribed by various vulnerabilities and disabilities. On the other side of the divide were their former masters, who frequently considered personal deference and elevated social recognition as nothing less than their rightful due, and thus sought to uphold their favoured social status for as long as possible.

In the case of labour, a widespread lack of faith in the efficiency of free labour markets saw economic elites in many parts of the globe turning to involuntary techniques in an effort to secure continuing supplies of cheap, reliable and ample labour. These practices were particularly significant in jurisdictions where slaves had previously played a major economic role, making it necessary to secure suitable replacements for labour that would otherwise have been supplied by slaves (Quirk, 2006, p. 591). For most former masters, the issue at stake was not so much maximizing profits, as minimizing losses (both past investments and future returns) stemming from legal abolition. Involuntary labour practices would range from crude forms of 'man catching' under colonial rule, where subject peoples were forcibly uprooted and compelled to labour on various projects, to more elaborate models based upon 'vagrancy' laws, penal labour, dubious labour contracts, forced labour for the state, indentured migration, bonded labour, a legal obligation to work, and even taxation, monetary and land policies. None of these techniques were necessarily new, but they would nonetheless acquire greater prominence in the wake of legal abolition (see Daniel, 1990; Holt, 1992, pp. 185, 202-204; Kloosterboer, 1960; Lasker, 1950; Miers, 2003, pp. 126-128, 135-141).

Of particular importance here are bonded labour, indentured servitude, and forced labour for the state. The key features of the relationship between slavery and bonded labour have been discussed in previous chapters. Indentured servitude involved millions of labourers from Asia, Africa, the Pacific and, especially, the Indian subcontinent being transported to many destinations to toil under highly restrictive contracts for extended periods (Northrup, 1995; Tickner, 1974). Forced labour for the state was usually more localized, as millions of people were pressed into service on many projects, routinely enduring horrific treatment, little or no payment, and high mortality (Cooper, 2000, pp. 129-149; Duffy, 1975, pp. 159-202). In some cases, these recruits closely followed in the footsteps of slaves, to the point of being housed in the same quarters. In parts of Africa, both French and Portuguese traders would buy slaves and then disingenuously rebrand them indentured labourers. In other cases, such as Peru, Malaya or Fiji, links with slavery are more tangential, with labourers being recruited from India, China and Japan. A similar story applies to forced labour. Under colonial rule slaves and ex-slaves were often the first to be pressed into service, but rapacious demands for labour also impacted upon 'native' peoples more generally.

The most notorious example here is the Congo Free State, where a multinational contingent under the authority of King Leopold of Belgium perpetrated numerous crimes against humanity over many decades. To maximize rubber profits, colonial agents would work to death (or simply murder) around ten million people, representing perhaps half of the total population (Grant, 2005, pp. 39-78; Hochschild, 1998, pp. 225-234). Tens of thousands who were fortunate enough to escape death would end up as cripples following a widespread practice of severing the limbs of communities and individuals who resisted. While this human catastrophe eventually aroused political opposition in some parts of Europe and North America, most critics tended to view the horrors of the Congo as a 'deviation' from, or 'exception' to, an otherwise legitimate colonial norm, instead of a symptom of the fundamental failings of European rule. It is now clear, however, that the Congo constitutes a particularly extreme example of broader patterns of behaviour that applied to both colonial Africa and colonial rule more broadly (Brantlinger, 2003; Hochschild, 1998, pp. 278-283)

In the specific case of forced labour, both private and public agents coerced Africans into service in many different settings, most notably when it came to the construction of railroads and agricultural production. The use of forced labour was also further exacerbated by frequent armed conflicts. During the First World War, millions of Africans were crudely forced into service as porters, transporting great burdens considerable distances for little or no reward. Tens of thousands would die on the battlefield, and of disease, starvation or exhaustion. Conscripted African soldiers (many of whom were slaves) also fought on fronts in Africa, Europe and the Middle East (Conklin, 1997, pp. 143-173; Klein, 1998, pp. 216-219, 233-235; Killingray, 1989).

Forced labour was a recurring feature of armed conflict in many parts of the globe throughout this period, and would be a core feature of various crimes against humanity committed by both public officials and private companies under Nazi rule between 1933 and 1945. This was not limited to the concentration camps which were central to the Holocaust (see Bloxham, 2001), but also extended to the extensive use of forced labour more generally. In August 1944, there were officially 7,615,970 foreign workers registered within the 'Greater German Reich', comprising around 1.9 million prisoners of war and 5.7 million civilian workers. This included 1.3 million French, 1.7 million Poles, and 2.8 million Soviet citizens. Around 12 million people were subject to Nazi forced labour during the Second World War (Herbert, 1997, p. 1; see also Gregor, 1998). Other serious abuses, albeit on a lesser scale, were also perpetrated by imperial Japan, most notably through the abuse of between 100,000 and 200,000 'comfort women' subjected to sexual servitude (Hicks, 1995; Yoshimi, 2001).

In the first half of the twentieth century, forced labour for the state was practised on a colossal scale, incorporating colonial exploitation, indigenous practices, systematic wartime abuses, and communist gulags. In the face of these global problems, the still widespread assumption that slavery ended in the nineteenth century appears appallingly complacent. In the additional case of Communist regimes in the Soviet Union, Eastern Europe, China and North Korea, thousands of forced labour camps were home to tens of millions of people forced into service under truly inhuman conditions. In the Soviet Union alone, these labour camps housed around 18 million people between 1929 and 1953 (when other forms of forced labour are included, the total increases to 28.7 million). At least 2.75 million people did not survive (Applebaum, 2003, pp. 515-522). These camps served a number of economic purposes, but their official rationale had more to do with ideological agendas than commercial considerations, providing a punitive platform for 'disciplining' and 're-educating' (suspected) ideological and political enemies. The use of forced labour by the state has steadily declined over the last half century, but remains a significant issue in countries such as North Korea and Myanmar (Chol-Hwan, 2001, pp. 47-154; Hawk, 2003, pp. 24-55). In one particularly egregious example, tens of thousands of North Koreans recently ended up in isolated work camps in Russian Siberia, enduring inhuman conditions as part of a bilateral deal to help repay Soviet era debt (Devalpo, 2006).

The Lasting Legacies of Historical Slave Systems

Viewed from a contemporary vantage point, there is no question that post-abolition practices have consistently left a great deal to be desired. However, it is also important to recognize that the tremendous obstacles involved in simply reaching the point where slavery was prohibited would also invariably circumscribe political possibilities in the aftermath of legal abolition. In some cases, the legal abolition of slavery (at least in the short-term) resulted in little or no substantive gains. In others, legal abolition resulted in a range of qualified yet still consequential improvements in overall levels of consumption, family integrity, economic remuneration, and personal autonomy and movement, together with a decline in some of the more heinous aspects of slavery, such as public auctions, the gang labour system, widespread slave raiding, and the horrors of trans-continental slave trading. While these gains clearly represent positive developments, they are also in turn massively compromised by the resort to – and independent continuation of – other forms of bondage. How should legal abolition be viewed in Africa, when colonial conquest brought about forced labour, multiple acts of genocide, and exploitation and destruction on a massive scale? To what extent is the closure of the Transatlantic slave trade undercut by the parallel growth of indentured migration? It is here that the divide between legal abolition and effective emancipation becomes particularly acute.

Some of these practices have declined over time. Others remain with us to this day, having been gradually incorporated under the rubric of contemporary slavery. Before going any further, however, it is also important to reflect upon another key piece of the puzzle: the enduring legacies of historical patterns of enslavement. This sensitive issue is chiefly associated with recent moves to seek reparations for slavery, but also extends to larger questions of recognition and representation. In the case of reparations, most energies have been devoted to two main issues: i) the legacies of slavery in the United States (Martin and Yaquinto, 2007), and ii) long-term relationships between European and African peoples (Howard-Hassmann, 2008). Many other aspects of the history of slavery have been largely overlooked. While a case can be made that other comparable practices should also be integrated into evolving discussions of reparations, efforts to incorporate neglected topics need to be motivated by genuine concerns about historical injustice, rather than by self-serving attempts to sidestep the discussion of restitution by pointing to problems elsewhere.

In both of the cases identified above, slavery has been placed alongside lasting patterns of discrimination, deprivation and exploitation. The problem at hand is not simply slavery in the United States and/or Transatlantic slavery, but also the systematic abuses associated with centuries of racial segregation and discrimination in the United States (and elsewhere), and the long-term impact of slavery and colonialism on Africa. The two main issues are: i) unjust enrichment, and ii) collective deprivation and discrimination.

Unjust enrichment is concerned with the tremendous wealth derived from slavery by various individuals, corporations and governments. Of particular interest here is the extent to which Atlantic commerce contributed to the British Industrial Revolution (see Williams, 1964; Inikori, 2002). While this connection continues to be disputed, it is difficult to escape the larger point that slavery was a key source of wealth, and that this wealth has frequently had lasting consequences.

Collective deprivation and discrimination is the other side of the coin, raising the difficult question of the detrimental consequences of Transatlantic slavery for African peoples and their descendants in the Americas. From this standpoint, historical practices can be connected to a host of serious contemporary problems, ranging from profound structural inequalities between European and African states, to racially defined disparities in both standards of living and collective psychology within various societies (see Brooks, 2004, pp. 36-97; Robinson, 2000, pp. 201-247; Manning, 1990, pp. 168-176). On this front, it is also worth noting that discrimination stemming from historical patterns of enslavement is not only a problem in the Americas, but also extends to parts of Africa, with descendants of slaves facing serious discrimination on a range of fronts, including both marriage practices and social recognition (ILO, 2005, pp. 42-43).

The movement for reparations for slavery has drawn inspiration from both successful claims for compensation for other grievous historical abuses, such as Nazi genocide and Second World War internment in northern America, and a parallel trend towards greater engagement with – and publicly apologizing for – specific acts of historical injustice (Gibney et al., 2008; Thompson, 2002). The influence of the former is especially apparent in a series of recent lawsuits in the United States seeking financial restitution from both government agents and a number of corporations. To date, these lawsuits have made limited headway, reflecting the serious procedural obstacles involved in putting together a successful case. Since slavery was legal at the time, and recent claimants are descendants, rather than direct victims, these forms of litigation face substantial difficulties under current laws. While recent lawsuits have undoubtedly provided a useful means of publicizing the modern legacies of slavery, they also run the risk of reducing the question of reparations to polarized disputes over monetary compensation, resulting in political deadlock (Torpey, 2006, pp. 128-132).

On this divisive issue, it is important to emphasize that the main focus of many recent proposals have revolved around collective improvements through avenues such as education, trust funds, and community development, rather than individual cash settlements. Viewed from a reparations perspective, developmental assistance ceases to be a discretionary exercise, or charitable contribution, and instead represents a compelling obligation which must be discharged in order to adhere to even minimum standards of ethical behaviour. For this perspective to command popular support, there needs to be greater public engagement when it comes to the history and legacies of slavery. In this context, a useful point of departure comes from Roy Brooks, who views the question of reparations through a framework of atonement and forgiveness, arguing that reparations can offer a framework for understanding and resolving the damaged political culture of the United States, with genuine atonement for past injustices serving as a vehicle for civic republicanism (Brooks, 2004, p. 170). For Brooks, a collective appreciation of the precise nature and scale of the historical injustices involved in slavery is an essential precondition for effective restitution:

> Clarification is desperately needed regarding the historical record on American slavery. The telling of this story has been the mother's milk of white misunderstanding about the peculiar institution and white complacency about its lingering effects. When whites reject reparations on the ground that they had nothing to do with slavery, they fail to understand the centrality of slavery in the socioeconomic development of this great country from which they benefit (Brooks, 2004, p. 148).

It is here that questions of recognition and representation become especially salient.

Without sufficient public recognition of the defining characteristics and consequences of slavery, it becomes difficult to mobilize sufficient political resources to address contemporary problems. When it comes to the question of historical legacies, three main challenges can be identified. First, we have the challenge of historical silence, where slavery often plays no part in how many past events have been represented. Once the absence of slavery is viewed as 'normal', rather than exceptional, it is easy for basic features of the history of slavery to disappear from public memory. As we have seen, slavery was a major part of the Ottoman Empire for centuries, yet in Turkey during the 1990s 'no day existed to commemorate abolition, and there were no references to the embarrassing institution in school textbooks' (Clarence-Smith, 2006, p. 110). In a number of cases, the primary issue is not the quality of public discourse regarding slavery, but the near total absence of any discourse at all. Second, we have a widespread tendency to reduce slavery to a peripheral feature, rather than a fundamental factor. One influential example of this dynamic comes from David Blight, who argues that reconciliation between north and south following the civil war in the United States involved, amongst other things, a common celebration of the martial heroism of white soldiers, and a common marginalization of the importance of slavery as a catalyst for conflict (Blight, 2001). Once slavery is viewed as a 'peculiar' anomaly, or temporary exception, it becomes easy to treat slavery as a marginal issue, instead of an integral foundation of social, economic and political life for thousands of years.

Finally, we have the challenge of balancing the history of slavery with the history of abolition. This is mainly an issue in Britain and the United States, where there remains a lingering tendency to chiefly focus upon the successful campaigns which culminated in legal abolition, rather than the many hundreds of years where slavery was practised without any meaningful opposition. One perspective on this long-standing disposition comes from John Oldfield, who observes that for much of the twentieth century:

> Britons – and Britain's colonial subjects – were taught
> to view transatlantic slavery though the moral triumph
> of abolition ... Whether seen through the lens of
> abolitionists relics or celebrations and commemorations,
> what is so often striking about this specific 'history' is
> its silèncing of African perspectives, and, in particular,
> the suffering of the millions who were sold into slavery
> (Oldfield, 2007, p. 2).

These types of representations not only minimize centuries of historical injustice, they also have a tendency to accentuate the achievements of legal abolition, leaving limited scope for difficult questions about subsequent shortcomings. While recent efforts to engage with the history of slavery in Britain have often displayed greater sensitivity to a number of these issues, collective recognition of the history and legacies of slavery has continued to be an uphill struggle (see also Rice, 2003, pp. 201-217; Wallace, 2006).

Contemporary Forms of Slavery

The four cases considered here concern India, Mauritania, Singapore, and Britain. Each of these cases is concerned with a different aspect of contemporary slavery: bonded labour, chattel slavery, migrant domestic labour, and trafficking in persons. Many countries could have potentially been included here, since equivalent patterns of behaviour can also be found in other jurisdictions, but these cases nonetheless offer a series of useful snapshots. In each of these countries we can point to a number of advances in recent times, but a great deal remains to be accomplished.

India

When India and Pakistan became independent states in 1947, political elites in both countries continued earlier colonial precedents sanctioning bonded labour. One of the clearest illustrations of fundamental official shortcomings is the length of time which passed before specific legislation against bonded labour was introduced. As we saw in Chapter One, bonded labour was one of four practices placed alongside slavery in the 1956 Supplementary Convention. The Indian Government was quick to sign this Convention, yet failed to pass national legislation for nearly 20 years, before finally introducing the Bonded Labour System (Abolition) Rules of 1976 (Pakistan and Nepal have even poorer records, with Nepal only legally abolishing bonded labour in 2000, despite having endorsed the 1956 Convention in 1963).

The 1976 Act has many excellent provisions, but implementation has consistently proved to be a major problem. Under the terms of the Act, bonded labour is defined in expansive terms as a system of forced or partly forced labour, where a debtor enters (or is presumed to have entered) into an agreement (oral or written) with a creditor, where an 'advance' compels the debtor (or any family members) to labour for either a specified or unspecified period (NCHE, 1990, pp. 3-8). Primary responsibility for enforcing the Act lies with District magistrates and their designated subordinates, but magistrates are often reluctant to report bonded labour, since any admission that a problem exists also means acknowledging their previous failures to take effective action (Bales, 1999, pp. 217-218; Coursen-Neff, 2003, p. 70). For years, various officials have been disingenuously claiming that bonded labour is no longer an issue within their particular jurisdictions (Srivastava, 2005, p. 7; Upadhyaya, 2004, pp. 133-134).

Instead of seeking out those in bondage, various officials have routinely placed the onus upon those in bondage to formally register their grievances. This is not feasible. Bonded labourers may not even be aware of relevant laws, and even if they are aware of their rights they often have every reason to expect that their complaints will be ignored, or simply invite retaliation. According to the 1976 Act, all debts associated with bonded labour should be immediately extinguished without compensation, but there have been consistent reports of officials endorsing debts as binding contracts which need to be repaid. This could stem from genuine confusion, but is more likely to reflect widespread corruption, as police have also been reported tracking down and returning runaways. Relatively few people have been prosecuted, let alone convicted or imprisoned, for employing bonded labour (Srivastava, 2003, p. 33). When successful interventions do occur, they are usually limited to release from bondage.

At this juncture, rehabilitation becomes essential. When bonded labourers in India are formally identified, they are entitled to resources administered through a centrally-sponsored scheme. This starts with a subsistence grant and may also include land allotments, the provision of animals, and/or tools and training, along with preferential treatment in development programmes (Nainta, 1997, pp. 94-95). The outcomes of these schemes have been mixed. Some promising results have been achieved (Bales, 2007, pp. 41-46, 62-68; Srivastava, 2005, pp. 18, 33-35), but much more need to be done. In some cases, relevant provisions have sometimes been inappropriate and/or late in arriving (Coursen-Neff, 2003, pp. 51-52, 71; Mishra, 2001, p. 19). A far larger problem, however, is that rehabilitation has only been experienced by a lucky minority, with funds being allocated for victims regularly going unspent. Despite these deficiencies, it is clear that rehabilitation programmes can make a decisive difference. In 2005, around 265,000 people were reported to have been involved in these ongoing schemes (Srivastava, 2005, p. 6). While this is undoubtedly a substantial figure, millions remain in bondage.

There is no shortage of material available on bonded labour in India (Mishra, 2002). In many cases, inquiries from different time periods are depressingly repetitive, with recent observers pointing to the same underlying issues which were highlighted in the 1970s, or even much earlier. Alongside the key issue of official complicity, numerous studies have also connected bonded labour to larger problems of caste-based discrimination, historical tradition, lack of land and other resources, access to credit, entrenched gender roles, and endemic poverty. These problems not only provide an explanation for why enslavement continues to be a widespread problem, they also help to explain ongoing official failures to take corrective action, as victims tend to be concentrated in marginalized groups lacking political and economic power.

Faced with these shortcomings, anti-slavery activists and other relevant groups (including the Indian Supreme Court), have ended up pursuing a combination of both direct and indirect approaches, with the former involving targeted action to release specific slaves at particular locations, and the latter revolving around long-term improvements in key areas such as levels of education, poverty reduction and social equality. While these larger reforms are clearly important, the importance attached to indirect models can also represent a politically attractive (i.e. less confrontational) alternative to direct intervention. More than 30 years after legislative reform, overall progress remains limited to modest gains, rather than major advances.

Mauritania

On 9 November 1981, the Government of Mauritania issued a public ordinance formally abolishing slavery throughout the country. This followed an earlier largely symbolic pronouncement on the 5 July 1980. These measures appear to have been provoked by protests over the public sale of a female slave (Cotton, 1998, pp. 30-31). The presence of slavery in Mauritania had not gone entirely unnoticed before 1980, but these two official proclamations attracted significant international interest, resulting in Mauritania acquiring a dubious reputation as the only country where 'widespread, institutionalized slavery persisted into the late 20th century' (Burkett, 1997, p. 57). This formula somewhat overstated matters – Niger (re) abolished slavery in 2003 and residual problems have also been reported elsewhere in Africa – but it nonetheless helped to attract significant international interest from journalists, activists and officials, resulting in a steady stream of missions, reports, exposés and public hearings.

Like most states in Africa, Mauritania is a European invention, having once been part of French West Africa. To placate their often rebellious subjects, French authorities left most aspects of local slave systems intact, while falsely claiming that slavery had effectively ended. This pattern continued following independence. Over the last half-century, this severely impoverished country has regularly experienced both national and international turmoil, enduring multiple coups d'état, communal violence and political repression. Many of these events revolve around enduring social cleavages, as Mauritania remains divided between 'White' Moors (Beidane), 'Black' Moors (Haratine) and 'African' tribes. The political and economic superiority of the 'White' Moors is chiefly based on the subjugation of their 'Black' counterparts, whose status is bound up in slavery. Having been conquered, captured and enslaved at various points in the past, these 'Black' Moors have taken on the culture of their masters.

The number of slaves in Mauritania has aroused considerable debate. One early estimate speaks of 'a minimum of 100,000 total slaves, with a further 300,000 part-slaves and ex-slaves' (Mercer, 1982, p. 1). More recent accounts have introduced a wide spectrum of estimates, with one local non-governmental organization suggesting that there may be as many as 600,000 slaves (BBC, 2007). These figures challenge decades of official declarations that the problem of slavery has been reduced to residual 'vestiges' of historical practices. This position has never been plausible. While the overall scale of the issues involved remains open to debate, there is no doubt that slavery has continued to be a widespread problem. Over the years, there have been a series of reports documenting the plight of individual slaves, chronicling torture, sexual abuse, systematic exploitation, arduous work routines, far-reaching official complicity, and the separation of families (ASI, 1992; AI, 2002; Fleischman, 1994). Many of these reports concern women. Slave trading (and kidnappings) have continued on a small scale, but provide only minor sources of new slaves. The vast majority of slaves have acquired their status at birth, making the viability of the system dependent on children born into slavery.

Slavery in Mauritania is not a static artefact, but a dynamic institution. In this context, a sophisticated analysis comes from Urs Peter Ruf, who points to a number of long-term adjustments in boundaries between masters and slaves. Alongside the serious abuses identified above, we also encounter reports of slaves and ex-slaves being well treated and establishing self-governing spaces. These outcomes are often not so much positive goods as lesser indignities, but they are nonetheless symptomatic of changing patterns of behaviour, as the historical prerogatives of a number of slave-holders appear to have been gradually diluted by various catalysts, including colonial policies, the crippling drought of the early 1970s, a disastrous war in Western Sahara, and the official proclamations in the early 1980s. Over time, these influences have had a cumulative but by no means uniform impact, with a number of slaves escaping from some of their more onerous obligations without overthrowing their servile status entirely (Ruf, 1999).

This does not mean, however, that slavery can be expected to inexorably fade away with the passage of time. One of the main sticking points here is the relationship between slavery and social hierarchy. This is partially a question of ingrained customs and orientations, and partially a question of political power. In the case of the former, we find 'a mental state of slavery: arrogance on the part of the former masters … and subservience on the part of … slaves and manumitted slaves' (Ruf, 1999, p. 10). In the case of the latter, we find a lasting pattern of dominance by 'White' Moors, which has manifested itself in various forms of caste based discrimination (Diallo, 1993). These social and political dynamics have not only helped to maintain slavery, they have also circumscribed opportunities for those of slave heritage, suggesting that social discrimination is likely to continue even if slavery itself finally comes to an end.

On this front, there have recently been a number of mixed indications, with a coup d'état in 2005 eventually paving the way for unprecedented multi-party elections in March 2007. This changing political climate (and emerging oil wealth) has made it possible to re-open the question of slavery. On 9 August 2007, the Mauritanian Parliament unanimously passed a new bill making slavery a criminal offence punishable by up to ten years in prison. Significantly, this new legislation also includes provisions modelled upon anti-Semitism laws in some European countries, prescribing a two-year prison term for the author of a cultural or artistic production that justifies or glorifies slavery. While these events are undoubtedly welcome developments, it remains to be seen whether they mark a decisive break with the past (Souaré, 2007). This uncertainty has recently been compounded by a coup against Prime Minister Yahia Ould Ahmed El-Waqef in August 2008. This has once again thrown Mauritania into turmoil, and it remains to be seen whether concerted anti-slavery efforts will continue in the face of renewed political instability.

Singapore

In places such as Mauritania and India, major concentrations of human bondage can be chiefly traced to absolute poverty, social discrimination, weak institutions, and historical legacies. In wealthy industrialized (and some oil-producing) countries, the situation tends to be somewhat different, with citizenship, economic returns, global inequality, and international migration instead constituting the main ingredients. Citizenship status is chiefly determined by accident of birth, but it nonetheless has profound consequences for individual life chances. Citizens of wealthy industrial countries can sometimes be enslaved, but these cases represent the exception, not the rule. Sadly, citizens of poorer countries tend to be far more vulnerable. As we have seen, this vulnerability is not confined to their countries of origin, but also extends to many citizens from poorer countries who seek to migrate to richer parts of the world, where their immigration status – or lack thereof – can increase their exposure to a spectrum of highly exploitative or otherwise problematic situations. Most of these cases do not amount to modern slavery, but situations which fall short of this standard still routinely leave a great deal to be desired. While there is no question that migration can be rewarding, in far too many cases the search for a better life tends to be defined by limited protections and high levels of vulnerability.

This dynamic is not limited to undocumented migration, where migrants do not have a legal right of residence, but also extends to millions of people who migrate legally, but who reside on restrictive terms which leave them vulnerable to forms of exploitation and abuse (Shelley, 2007). Of particular salience here is the globalization of migrant domestic work. This is now a leading sector for female employment across the globe, building upon growing demand for cleaners and carers within private households (see Anderson, 2000 and 2004; Ehrenreich and Hochschild, 2002). It also represents a major child labour issue, with many domestic labourers starting at a very young age (Blagbrough, 2008; Coursen-Neff and Bochenek, 2004). Global demand for domestic workers can be met through either national or international channels. In the case of the latter, extensive networks have emerged to recruit, place and police substantial flows of migrants from poorer countries. In some cases, domestic workers can also travel as part of diplomatic missions, leaving them especially vulnerable.

These networks have contributed to a marked growth in unaccompanied female migration, which is reported to be:

> particularly pronounced in the Philippines, Indonesia and Sri Lanka, where national-level estimates indicate that women comprise 60-75 percent of legal migrants. The vast majority of these are employed as domestic workers in the Middle East, Singapore, Malaysia and Hong Kong. Of the estimated 850,000 workers from Indonesia and Sri Lanka in Saudi Arabia, the majority are women and in some cases girls (using falsified travel documents) employed as domestic workers. There are approximately 160,000 migrant domestic workers in Singapore and 300,000 in Malaysia (Sunderland and Varia, 2006, p. 3; see also Brown and Saunders, 2004; Ally, 2005)

Being concentrated in the home, domestic workers tend to be excluded from many rights and protections that govern labour relations more generally, building on the notion that private homes fall under different standards to other workplaces.

As the preceding snapshot makes clear, the case of Singapore is by no means isolated, but recent events nonetheless help to shed light upon larger global trends. Female migration into Singapore is not an entirely new phenomenon, but can be found under British colonial rule during the first half of the twentieth century (Chiang, 1994). Domestic work more generally has a much longer historical pedigree, having been an integral feature of life in privileged households for thousands of years. It is clear, however, that cheap air travel, economic inequalities and commercial calculations have paved the way for a number of distinctively modern innovations. In an increasingly integrated world, migrant domestic labourers in Singapore now come from a wide range of countries, as political elites in places such as Indonesia, the Philippines, Sri Lanka, India, Bangladesh, Pakistan, and Thailand have increasingly promoted labour migration as a means of reducing unemployment, generating foreign exchange, and fostering economic growth. The regional leader here is the Philippines, where overseas contract workers comprised an estimated 7.4 million people in 2001. This constitutes close to 10 per cent of the population and 21 per cent of the total labour force (Cheah, 2006, p. 187), and results in a major economic contribution which can complicate efforts at regulation, as robust legal protections and advocacy could potentially undermine the attractiveness of Philippine migrants.

For some migrant workers, problems begin at the point of recruitment. With upwards of 600 agencies involved in bringing workers to Singapore, competition can be intense, so it is not uncommon for recruiters to turn to deceptive and abusive practices, with unlicensed agents often proving to be the worst offenders. To increase their returns, agents routinely seek to pass the transportation costs onto their clients, imposing substantial fees, 'private loans', and salary deductions (Varia, 2005, pp. 18-23). From a Singaporean perspective, domestic workers mainly fall under the jurisdiction of the Ministry of Manpower. Under existing legislation, domestic workers are excluded from the provisions of the Employment Act, which establishes a series of minimum standards of employment, and the Workmen's Compensation Act, which covers workplace injuries and occupational illness. They are instead governed by the Foreign Workers Act and the Employment Agencies Act, which offer more qualified terms and conditions structured around two-year work visas which make it difficult to change employers, and also prohibits pregnancy and 'breaking up families'. This legislation was strengthened in 2005 following adverse publicity surrounding abuses of migrant workers, but many restrictive provisions remain in place. Of particular importance here is a 5,000 Singaporean Dollar security bond, which employers must take out in order to guarantee that they will repatriate their domestic workers. This bond is forfeited if the worker runs away and seeks to stay on in Singapore illegally, creating strong incentives for employers to closely monitor their employees.

One in every six households in Singapore is said to employ a domestic worker in their home. Isolated within these private households, migrant domestic workers routinely experience a host of physical and psychological abuses, enduring long and irregular working hours, demeaning treatment, arbitrary punishments, sexual advances, poor pay and working conditions, and restrictions on movement. Migrant domestic workers in Singapore have reported working 13 to 19 hours a day, 7 days a week, without being able to leave their place of employment. For these arduous labours, they 'typically earn less than half the pay that workers earn in similar occupations in Singapore – such as gardening and cleaning – and are forced to relinquish the first four to ten months of their salaries to repay employment agency fees' (Varia, 2005, p. 2). At least 147 migrant workers are said to have died from workplace accidents or suicide between 1999 and 2005, with most jumping or falling from residential buildings. Singaporean authorities have regularly prosecuted particularly severe cases of abuse, but even practices which adhere to the letter of the law still regularly leave a great deal to be desired. When individuals exercise such high levels of discretionary authority over their employees, the best outcome that most migrant domestic workers can reasonably hope for is to be placed with a benevolent employer.

The growth of migrant domestic workers can be closely connected to the increased profile of Singaporean women, both economically and socially. As the female labour force participation rate has increased, so have numbers of migrant workers, moving from 40,000 in 1988 to more than 140,000 in 2001, with a 19 per cent increase between 1998 and 2001. In this environment, a strong case can be made that:

> '[t]he advancement and development of ... professional women ... thus involves a certain inhumanity: the bringing into the home of a foreign stranger who is dehumanized because she inherits the feminized chores of the wife and mother without any of their human-redemptive elements' (Cheah, 2006, p. 206; see also Anderson, 2000, pp. 9-27).

Framed in these terms, the enduring divide between privileged citizen and migrant outsider becomes difficult to avoid. As long as migrant domestic workers are viewed as temporary commodities rather than equal citizens deserving of core protections and entitlements, effective regulation and recognition will remain an uphill struggle.

Britain

Much like Singapore, recent events in Britain offer a fairly representative snapshot of some of the main issues and agendas revolving around contemporary slavery in wealthy industrialized countries. In Britain, as in many richer parts of the globe, the main concern has been human trafficking. While a limited amount of trafficking takes place within Britain, the vast majority of cases involve international migration. Of particular importance here is a recent influx of workers from Eastern Europe following the further expansion of the European Union (Portes and French, 2005; Branigan and

Wintour, 2007), but migrants have also arrived in significant numbers from other parts of the globe. While highly-skilled workers regularly secure substantial rewards, significant problems have been identified at the lower end of the labour market, with tens of thousands of migrants experiencing severe exploitation.

In keeping with larger trends, the two main issues in Britain have been sexual servitude and labour exploitation, with the former attracting the most attention. In the case of sexual servitude, one recent estimate tentatively suggests that at least 10,000 women and between 3,000 and 4,000 children have been trafficked into Britain for the purposes of sexual exploitation over the last decade. Anecdotal accounts suggest that many women end up trapped in servitude by responding to advertisements offering attractive jobs, or even offers of marriage. Many children have been trafficked with the compliance of family members. To ensure obedience, traffickers regularly make use of debt-bondage, deception, psychological manipulation, isolation and confinement, and threats, violence and vulnerability (Craig et al., 2007, pp. 40, 48-51; Joint Committee on Human Rights, 2006, pp. 28-35; Waugh, 2007, pp. 154-167). While outright corruption is much less of an issue in Britain than in most countries, a number of public agencies have been criticized for failing to identify victims and/or offer effective sanctuary. In a recent report on trafficking, 48 out of 80 documented cases of known or suspected victims of child trafficking involved children who later went missing from the care of social services and could not be located (Beddoe, 2007, pp. 20-22).

Trafficking for the purposes of labour exploitation has been documented in a wide range of settings. In a 2006 survey, forced labour was reported in agriculture, construction, domestic work, food processing and packaging, care/nursing, hospitality and the restaurant trade. The majority of victims entered the country legally, with traffickers making use of debt-bondage, the removal of relevant documents, and the uncertainty of many migrants about their residency status to exploit their labour (Skrivánková, 2006, pp. 14-16). Another parallel issue here once again is the exploitation of migrant domestic workers within private households, which echoes experiences in Singapore and elsewhere. Migrant domestic workers in Britain also usually enter the country legally under restricted visas (which may soon be restricted further), accompanying wealthy businessmen, visiting families, and expatriate families returning from overseas (Anderson, 2004). As is usually the case in such matters, all of these industries involve a spectrum of practices, with many workers being employed according to relevant statutes governing wages and conditions, while others experience serious abuses. There are an estimated 1.4 million registered foreign workers in Britain, with perhaps a further 300,000 to 800,000 migrants working illegally (Craig et al., 2007, p. 22). Only a small portion of this total are subject to modern slavery, but the exploitation and abuse of migrants once again remains a much larger phenomenon, with migrants routinely labouring under terms and conditions which few British citizens would readily accept (Skrivánková, 2007).

The profile of human trafficking in Britain has increased dramatically over the last ten years, resulting in a level of public and political engagement unseen since the late nineteenth and early twentieth century (see Walkowitz, 1982). This has been gradually reflected in government policies. Like many of its international peers, the British Government has recently tightened laws pertaining to trafficking, moving from a situation where trafficking was indirectly covered by various statutes, to a situation where trafficking is a specific offence with substantial penalties (Pearson, 2002, pp. 105-118; Skrivánková, 2006, pp. 10-12). Another new innovation is the Gangmasters (Licensing) Act 2004, which establishes a system for registering labour providers in agricultural, shellfish gathering and associated packing and processing industries.

Perhaps the most significant development in recent times has been the foundation of the United Kingdom Trafficking Centre in 2006, following a major operation targeting sexual exploitation which resulted in 232 people being arrested and 84 trafficking victims being identified and rescued (Joint Committee on Human Rights, 2006, p. 43). A network of support services has also recently been developed in order to provide sanctuary and help with rehabilitation, but more needs to be done in this area (Craig et al., 2007, pp. 52, 58-61; Skrivánková, 2006, pp. 13-14, and 2007, pp. 219-223). Unlike India or Mauritania, where lack of effective official action remains a major issue, the British Government has substantial resources at its disposable that can be called upon to take action. The key obstacle, however, remains the tremendous profits that can be derived from human trafficking. According to one recent estimate, the average annual profit from commercial sexual exploitation across industrialized countries was around 67,200 US dollars per victim of trafficking. This total greatly exceeds profits in other parts of the globe (Belser, 2005, p. 15). The economic logic here suggests that human trafficking is always going to be a difficult problem to effectively suppress.

Conclusion: Public Policy and Political Activism

The pioneers of organized anti-slavery worked towards an overarching goal: the legal abolition of slavery. This was a difficult, momentous undertaking, which challenged a global institution which had been an integral part of social order for thousands of years. Following many setbacks and false starts, this long-standing goal has finally been accomplished, with every country in the world now having legally abolished slavery.

The main sticking point, however, is how we approach this achievement. If slavery has been legally prohibited, but its more heinous characteristics have continued under a variety of different designations, or through numerous illicit activities, on what grounds can we say that slavery has effectively come to an end? If enslavement remains a fundamental issue in the absence of official recognition, on what grounds can we meaningfully distinguish chattel slavery from analogous forms of behaviour?

In this environment, the anti-slavery agenda has been caught up in a further series of analytical and political challenges, where the problems at hand are rarely amenable to sweeping legislative action, but instead require many overlapping strategies. Viewed from a public policy perspective, four main themes can be identified here: i) education, information and awareness; ii) further legal reform; iii) effective enforcement; and iv) release, rehabilitation and restitution. These themes represent the core of modern anti-slavery activism, offering a series of targeted improvements which should hopefully command support from a range of political and ideological perspectives. Over the last decade, there has been a marked improvement in the profile of human bondage, together with concurrent advances in anti-slavery activism and overall levels of official engagement. It is also clear, however, that a tremendous amount remains to be accomplished. This is partially a question of ongoing failures on a number of fronts, and partially a question of the intractable nature of many of the issues involved. Much like global poverty and environmental degradation, efforts to address most forms of contemporary slavery tend to be geared towards cumulative reductions in their overall scale and severity, rather than a single, decisive solution.

Education, Information and Awareness

The first plank in this political platform revolves around education, information and public awareness. Without an adequate appreciation of the defining characteristics and consequences of slavery, both past and present, it can be difficult to mobilize various constituencies to take effective remedial action. One of the most important issues here is the neglected relationship between historical practices and contemporary problems. Discussion of contemporary issues often takes place in a historical vacuum, leaving a range of important connections and associations out of the equation. When current problems are detached from the lessons and legacies of earlier political contests over slavery and servitude in various parts of the globe, we can end up with an incomplete diagnosis of both the problems at hand and the past history of efforts to address them.

One of the most effective ways of improving general knowledge about slavery is through public education. This starts with national education programmes, where the study of slavery, both past and present, should be introduced as a mandatory requirement. As this book makes clear, slavery is one of the most important themes in human history, having been practiced by most peoples at most times across the globe, yet this centrality and longevity is not reflected in most national education programmes. Of particular importance here is the relationship between the global and the local, where the study of slavery in individual locations or regions needs to be embedded within a larger historical framework, introducing a coherent global vision that provides a platform from which to explore local issues in more depth. On this front, it is important to place more familiar treatments of Transatlantic slavery alongside less familiar themes, such as slavery in the Middle East, Africa or the Indian Ocean. Slavery has always been a global issue. It should also be taught as a global issue.

Another valuable forum for education and information revolves around public heritage, where more can be done to raise overall awareness of the role of various slave systems in shaping the modern world. In his influential treatment of reparations, Roy Brooks puts forward a strong case for the construction of slavery museums in the United States, arguing that dedicated museums would provide an invaluable focal point for public discussion and dissemination concerning the history and legacies of slavery (Brooks, 2001, pp. 157-159). While this proposal requires careful implementation, the basic idea has considerable merit. Many major historical slave states, such as Portugal, Turkey and India, could also be encouraged to move in a similar direction, making a concerted effort to challenge enduring silences surrounding their own historical records when it comes to slavery. In this context, the primary goal is not simply to raise awareness of the history of slavery, but to draw upon gradual improvements in public awareness to help refine and further reinforce evolving efforts to confront both contemporary slavery and enduring historical legacies. When specific problems come to light, or specific human rights campaigns are set in motion, it is essential to have informed constituencies which can be called upon to support the anti-slavery cause.

The question of education and information also extends to various government agents, which also require specialized training in order to help identify victims, successfully prosecute offenders, and provide for rehabilitation. In countries where corruption and indifference remain widespread, there is a particular need for specialized agencies which can operate outside normal channels. The anti-slavery teams recently introduced in Brazil may offer a model here (Bales, 2007, pp. 120-126). This also extends to the issue of prevention, where it is also necessary to disseminate information to combat the deceptive techniques used by various 'recruiters'. Warnings against entrapment have featured in recent anti-trafficking campaigns, but they sometimes appear to be geared towards keeping prospective migrants at home, rather than ensuring they can migrate safely. Information on potential hazards will always be valuable, but when there are few attractive alternatives available it may simply end up clarifying the risks involved.

Education and information provide an essential foundation for many different endeavours. To maximize their influence, further research is essential. Over the last ten years, the study of slavery has experienced something of a renaissance, with scholars of slavery producing many valuable works, especially when it comes to the study of slavery outside the Americas. A similar growth pattern is also evident in the case of contemporary forms of slavery, with the volume of modern research increasing markedly in recent times, especially when it comes to human trafficking (Quirk, 2007, p. 193). While significant research continues to be required in both fields, past and present practices have tended to be viewed as independent topics, rather than overlapping and/or interrelated fields of study. To date, limited energy has been devoted to the comparative analysis of historical practices and modern problems.

Legal Reform and Regulation

The second plank in this political platform involves further legal reform. In recent times, there have been a number of efforts to refine relevant laws, close loopholes, toughen penalties, and regulate practices that can otherwise degenerate into slavery. These efforts need to be extended and further refined. Several key issues can be identified here, starting with the need to strengthen existing criminal sanctions. A good example here is the problem of human trafficking. Throughout the twentieth century, trafficking was rarely treated as a specific offence, but would instead be covered indirectly as part of more general injunctions dealing with issues such as prostitution or kidnapping. Over the last decade, many countries have introduced anti-trafficking legislation, making it easier (at least on paper) to pursue successful criminal prosecutions. This trend needs to be expanded, particularly when it comes to labour exploitation, where penalties can be surprisingly lenient, notwithstanding the seriousness of the offences involved. One notable example here is bonded labour in the Indian subcontinent, where masters can usually expect (at worst) modest fines for keeping people in bondage. Laws against slavery and servitude need to be clear, comprehensive, and contain appropriate penalties for abuses which amount to crimes against humanity under international law.

Another related theme involves better regulation. The overall goal here is not outright prohibition, but effective supervision. This dynamic applies to many different practices, including marriage, adoption, domestic workers, prison labour, child labour, migrant workers, and the recruitment of soldiers. All of these activities are legitimate in many circumstances, yet they can also be subject to a range of abuses. Each practice involves different challenges, making it difficult to offer general recommendations, but the basic rule of thumb is to offer protection against vulnerability, enhance the role of consent, introduce appropriate penalties for breaching regulations, and provide effective avenues to safely report abuses once they occur. When it comes to labour issues, legislative change often needs to be part of a larger package of reforms, which include specific provisions for regular workplace inspections and the certification of relevant employers. This can be difficult to achieve in irregular and illicit settings, but there remain many areas where better regulation can still make a valuable contribution.

Further legal reform also extends to the issue of confiscation and financial penalties. A number of forms of contemporary slavery regularly produce tremendous economic returns. Efforts to combat these practices could be enhanced by legal provisions to appropriate these criminal earnings. While some mechanisms already exist in several jurisdictions, further progress can be made here. On this front, it may also be worth extending serious financial penalties to individuals and corporations who make use of various goods and services produced by slaves. This is a contentious issue, but the returns associated with slavery have to come from somewhere. If those paying for slave products know – or could reasonably have been expected to know – of their origins, they should also be subject to financial penalties, if not criminal sanctions.

Effective Enforcement

The third plank in this core platform is effective enforcement. Existing laws may not be perfect, but their specific content means relatively little if they are not effectively enforced. As we have seen, this has been a widespread, long-standing problem. Throughout history, there have been few (if any) serious repercussions for even the most heinous, systematic abuses. This is largely a testament to widespread government involvement. Most historical abuses have taken place because of, rather than in spite of, official endeavours. This pervasive lack of accountability has continued to this day. While it is not unheard of for slaves to escape through either personal action or external intervention, this does not necessarily mean that those who enslaved them will face meaningful criminal sanctions. Bonded labourers on the Indian subcontinent have been freed, slaves and ex-slaves in Mauritania have fostered new opportunities, victims of trafficking have found refuge, yet their former masters have rarely been prosecuted. This widespread impunity ensures that masters in many jurisdictions have little fear of serious penalties for their predatory behaviour. This is not simply a question of official complicity, but also extends to widespread indifference to the plight of social outsiders, along with more familiar manpower, training and resource shortages.

There are no easy answers to these larger structural problems, but even a small number of successful prosecutions resulting in substantial penalties would pose a direct challenge to this culture of impunity. Even modest improvements in the overall capacity of relevant officials to enforce relevant laws would make a crucial difference. This is not, however, a problem which is easily reducible to specific concerns about anti-slavery, but also requires a much broader commitment to organizational reform.

Release, Rehabilitation and Restitution

The final plank in the platform involves release, rehabilitation and restitution. These can be loosely conceptualized as a series of phases, with escape from slavery serving as a starting point for a gradual process of recovery. This is a very difficult issue. Historically, escape from slavery has been confined to release, with slaves receiving little assistance beyond a formal change in legal status. This pattern has continued to this day. At this point in time, formal provisions for rehabilitation only cover a limited subset of involved persons, leaving a majority of slaves to fend for themselves. This is not simply a matter of cases escaping the notice of relevant officials. When slaves do come to official notice, they regularly end up being detained, returned, deported or hastily discharged, with little or no concern for their overall welfare or past history. Without adequate support, former slaves can tragically end up being re-enslaved. In this environment, all governments need to make provisions for rehabilitation a priority.

In light of these failures, slaves who end up in rehabilitation schemes can be fortunate to receive any support at all. It is clear, however, that current provisions for rehabilitation remain a work in progress. Some states have recently introduced special dispensations for international trafficking victims, but these sometimes come with a number of strings attached, ensuring that not everyone will be eligible for assistance. The Indian Government has introduced commendable schemes for rehabilitation, but this support can sometimes be unsuitable and/or slow in coming. With even the best will in the world, rehabilitation will always be an expensive, time consuming process, since traumatized individuals require both material support and psychological fortification. On this front, the history of both pre- and post-abolition resistance potentially offers an instructive precedent. As we have seen, slaves and former slaves have consistently pursued a variety of goals in the face of tremendous challenges. The purpose of rehabilitation schemes should be to fortify these remarkable tendencies, offering sufficient support for the agency and autonomy of former slaves to flourish.

The question of restitution revolves around the long-term legacies of enslavement. To date, discussion has chiefly focused upon claims for monetary damages arising from selected slave systems, but this is by no means the only strategy available here (HRW, 2001). In its most basic form, restitution revolves around a genuine recognition of the precise nature of the wrong which has been committed, and a sincere attempt to make restitution for past injustices. This means placing slavery alongside ongoing problems of social discrimination and economic deprivation. Once we go beyond immediate perpetrators, the issues at stake usually involve broader communities, rather than specific individuals. In this environment, two basic principles should apply: i) restitution should apply at a collective, rather than individual level; and ii) the main focus should be addressing current problems, rather than compensating past sufferings. Discussion of reparations for historical slave systems have rarely engaged with the issue of modern slavery, but there is potentially scope for a more integrated perspective here. Since most governments and communities have such poor historical records when it comes to human bondage, one way in which they can help to redress earlier shortcomings is to renew their efforts to combat contemporary forms of slavery.

A Question of Vision

The overall efficacy of this core political platform will always be at least partially contingent upon the relationship between targeted improvements and underlying structural dynamics. Long-standing failures to enforce relevant anti-slavery laws are not simply a matter of individual failings, but can also be traced to prevailing social mores, political considerations, institutional weakness, and vested economic interests. From this vantage point, the specific issue of slavery will always be bound up in larger political and institutional problems. A similar story also applies to other structural problems, covering issues such as caste, poverty, gender, demography, land reform and social roles. Improvements on any of these fronts can be expected to have an important – albeit largely indirect – impact upon the scope and severity of contemporary slavery.

In any discussion of contemporary slavery, poverty is consistently identified as an essential factor, as vulnerability, desperation and a lack of viable alternatives clearly make a major contribution to modern problems. If we are serious about contemporary slavery, we also need to be serious about reducing poverty, but this does not make it any easier to reach an agreement on how to advance this fundamental goal, or to make the types of sacrifices required as part of a genuine commitment to improve the lives of the most vulnerable. If we are serious about confronting both contemporary slavery and enduring historical legacies, we also need to develop a global vision which places slavery alongside larger questions of poverty, inequality, racism and discrimination. Much like questions of gender and the environment, every relevant policy document, planning meeting, political platform and commercial enterprise should include an explicit anti-slavery component, with the impact of various policies and activities being directly evaluated according to their capacity to combat contemporary slavery.

In his most recent work, Kevin Bales touches upon the idea of vision, observing that many people fail to see the slavery which surrounds us (Bales, 2007, p. 53). While this is partially a question of widespread complacency, there is also a deeper inheritance at work here. Over the last two and a half centuries, slavery has come to be construed as a (somewhat) regrettable feature of an earlier, less developed stage in human evolution. When slavery is approached as an historical relic, rather than a dynamic problem, blindness to contemporary problems is to be expected. To overthrow this cultural inheritance, a deeper and broader vision is required. Rather than reducing slavery to a 'peculiar' historical anomaly (to be explained away), we instead need to view slavery as a widespread and deeply rooted component of contemporary life.

Bibliography

International Conventions

Abolition of Forced Labour Convention (No. 105). 1957. Available at
    http://www.ohchr.org/english/law/abolition.htm.

Convention on the Rights of the Child. 1989. Available at
    http://www.ohchr.org/english/law/crc.htm.

*Convention for the Suppression of the Traffic in Persons and of the Exploitation
    of the Prostitution of Others*. 1949. Available at
    http://www.ohchr.org/english/law/trafficpersons.htm.

Forced Labour Convention (No. 29). 1930. Available at
    http://www.ohchr.org/english/law/forcedlabour.htm.

*Protocol to Prevent, Suppress and Punish Trafficking in Persons Especially
    Women and Children, supplementing the United Nations Convention
    against Transnational Organized Crime*. 2000. Available at
    http://www.ohchr.org/english/law/protocoltraffic.htm.

*Slavery, Servitude, Forced Labour and Similar Institutions and Practices
    Convention*. 1926. Available at
    http://www.ohchr.org/english/law/slavery.htm.

*United Nations Supplementary Convention on the Abolition of Slavery, the
    Slave Trade and Institutions, and Practices Similar to Slavery*. 1956.
    Available at http://www.ohchr.org/english/law/slavetrade.htm.

Worst Forms of Child Labour Convention (No. 182). 1999. Available at
    http://www.ohchr.org/english/law/childlabour.htm.

Reports and News Articles

Ally, S. 2005. *Always on Call: Abuse and Exploitation of Child Domestic
    Workers in Indonesia*. New York, Human Rights Watch.

Amnesty International. 2002. *Mauritania: A Future Free from Slavery?*
    38/003/2002. Available at
    http://web.amnesty.org/library/pdf/AFR380032002ENGLISH/$File/
    AFR3800302.pdf, accessed on 28 October 2007.

An Approach to Reparations, Human Rights Watch Position Paper. 2001. Available at http://www.hrw.org/english/docs/2001/07/19/global284.htm, accessed on 22 October 2007.

Asian Development Bank. 2003. *Combating Trafficking of Women and Children in South Asia: Regional Synthesis Paper for Bangladesh, India, and Nepal*. Available at http://www.adb.org/Documents/Books/Combating_Trafficking/ Regional_Synthesis_Paper.pdf, accessed on 25 September 2007.

BBC. 2007. Mauritanian MPs Pass Slavery Law. 2007. *BBC News Online*, 9 August. Available at http://news.bbc.co.uk/2/hi/africa/6938032.stm, accessed on 27 October 2007.

Beddoe, C. 2007. *Missing Out: A Study of Child Trafficking in the North-West, North-East and West Midlands*. London, ECPAT UK. Available at http://www.ecpat.org.uk/downloads/ECPAT_UK_Missing_Out_2007. pdf, accessed on 31 October 2007.

Belser, P. 2005. *Forced Labour and Human Trafficking: Estimating the Profits*. Geneva, International Labour Office. Available at http://www.ilo.org/wcmsp5/groups/public/---ed_norm/--- declaration/documents/ publication/wcms_081971.pdf, accessed on 25 September 2007.

Blagbrough, J. 2008. *'They Respect their Animals More': Voices of Child Domestic Workers*. London, Anti-Slavery International.

Bonded Labour and its Abolition, Volume Two: Documents; Part 1, Statutes, Reports and Circulars. 1990. New Delhi, National Centre for Human Settlement and Environment.

Branigan, T. and Wintour, P. 2007. Ministers Ignored Calls to Improve Migration Figures. *The Guardian Online*, 31 October. Available at http://www.guardian.co.uk/immigration/story/0,,2202144,00.html, accessed on 31 October 2007.

Brown, W. and Saunders, J. (eds) 2004. *Bad Dreams: Exploitation and Abuse of Migrant Workers in Saudi Arabia*. New York, Human Rights Watch.

Burkett, E. 1997. God Created Me To Be a Slave. *New York Times Magazine*. 12 October.

Coursen-Neff, Z. 2003. *Small Change: Bonded Child Labor in India's Silk Industry*. 2003. New York, Human Rights Watch. Available at http://www.hrw.org/reports/2003/india/india0103.pdf, accessed on 28 October 2007.

Coursen-Neff, Z. and Bochenek, M. 2004. *Abuses Against Child Domestic Workers in El Salvador*. New York, Human Rights Watch.

Department of State. 2008. *Trafficking in Persons Report, June 2008*. 2008. US Department of State. Available at http://www.state.gov/documents/organization/105501.pdf, accessed on 21 August, 2008.

Gould, C. 2008. *Selling Sex in Cape Town. Sex Work and Human Trafficking in a South African City*. Institute for Security Studies, available at http://www.issafrica.org/index.php?link_id=3&slink_id=6167&link_type=12&slink_type=12&tmpl_id=3, accessed on 21 August, 2008.

Craig, G. Gaus, A. Wilkinson, M. Skrivánková, K. and McQuade, A. 2007. *Contemporary Slavery in the UK: Overview and Key Issues*. York, Joseph Rowntree Foundation. Available at http://www.jrf.org.uk/bookshop/eBooks/2016-contemporary-slavery-UK.pdf, accessed on 31 October 2007.

Data Comparison Sheet #1 (Volume 2), Worldwide Trafficking Estimates by Organizations. *UNESCO Trafficking Statistics Project*. Available at http://www.unescobkk.org/fileadmin/user_upload/culture/Trafficking/statdatabase/Worldwide_Estimates_Feb2008.pdf, accessed on 28 November 2008.

Devalpo, A. 2006. North Korean Slaves: Russia's Imported Koretsky Labour without Reward. *Le Monde Diplomatique*, April 2006. Available at http://mondediplo.com/2006/04/08koreanworkers, accessed on 28 October 2007.

Dufka, C. 2005. *Youth, Poverty and Blood: The Lethal Legacy of West Africa's Regional Warriors*. New York, Human Rights Watch. Available at http://hrw.org/reports/2005/westafrica0405/westafrica0405.pdf, accessed on 27 September 2007.

Fleischman, J. 1994. *Mauritania's Campaign of Terror: State-Sponsored Repression of Black Africans*. New York, Human Rights Watch/Africa.

Hawk, D. 2003. *The Hidden Gulag: Exposing North Korea's Prison Camps, Prisoners' Testimonies and Satellite Photographs.* Washington, U.S. Committee for Human Rights in North Korea. Available at http://www.hrnk.org/HiddenGulag.pdf, accessed on 28 October 2007.

Human Rights Watch. 2003. *Abducted and Abused: Renewed Conflict in Northern Uganda. 2003.* New York, Human Rights Watch/Africa. Available at http://www.hrw.org/reports/2003/uganda0703/, accessed on 14 September 2007.

Human Trafficking. Joint Committee on Human Rights. Twenty-Sixth Report of Session 2005-06. London, The Stationery Office Limited. Available at http://www.kalayaan.org.uk/documents/Human%20Rights%20 report.pdf, accessed on 1 November 2007.

ILO. 2002. *Every Child Counts: New Global Estimates on Child Labour.* 2002. Geneva, International Labour Office, available at http://www.ilo.org, accessed on 11 September 2007.

ILO. 2005. *A Global Alliance Against Forced Labour: Global Report Under the Follow-up to the ILO Declaration on Fundamental Principles and Rights at Work.* 2005. Geneva, International Labour Office. Available at http://www.ilo.org/dyn/declaris/DECLARATIONWEB.DOWNLOAD_ BLOB?Var_DocumentID=5059, accessed on 11 September 2007.

ILO. 2006. *The End of Child Labour: Within Reach. Global Report under the Follow-up to the ILO Declaration on Fundamental Principles and Rights at Work.* 2006. Geneva, International Labour Office. Available at http://www.ilo.org, accessed on 11 September 2007.

Joseph, W. 2007. Probe of Darfur 'Slavery' Starts. *BBC News.* Available at http://news.bbc.co.uk/2/hi/africa/6468097.stm, accessed on 27 September 2007.

Kelly, L. 2005. *Fertile Fields: Trafficking in Persons in Central Asia.* Vienna, International Organization for Migration. Available at http://www.belgium.iom.int/pan-europeandialogue/documents/ TRAFFICKING%20 IN%20PERSONS%20IN%20CENTRAL%20ASIA.pdf, accessed on 25 September 2007.

League of Nations. Dispute between Ethiopia and Italy. 1935. C.340.M.171.1935.VII, Geneva, 11 September, 1935.

Markon, J. 2007. Human Trafficking Evokes Outrage, Little Evidence: U.S. Estimates Thousands of Victims, But Efforts to Find Them Fall Short. *Washington Post*, Sunday, 23 September, 2007. Available at http://www.washingtonpost.com/wp-dyn/content/article/2007/09/22/AR2007092201401_pf.html, accessed on 21 August 2008.

Matsuura, K. 2003. *Message from the Director-General of UNESCO on the Occasion of the International Year to Commemorate the Struggle against Slavery and its Abolition (2004)*. Available at http://portal.unesco.org/culture/en/ev.php-URL_ID=17528&URL_DO=DO_TOPIC& URL_ SECTION=201.html, accessed on 13 September 2007.

Mishra, L. 2001. *A Perspective Plan to Eliminate Forced Labour in India*. Geneva, International Labour Office. Available at http://www.ilo.org/dyn/declaris/DECLARATIONWEB.DOWNLOAD_BLOB?Var_DocumentID=1548, accessed on 28 October 2007.

Mishra, L. 2002. *Annotated Bibliography on Forced/Bonded Labour in India*. Geneva, International Labour Office. Available at http://www.ilo.org/dyn/declaris/DECLARATIONWEB.DOWNLOAD_BLOB?Var_DocumentID=1556, accessed on 28 October 2007.

Ould, D. Jordan, C. Reynolds, R. and Loftin, L. 2004. T*he Cocoa Industry in West Africa: A History of Exploitation*. London, Anti-Slavery International. Available at http://www.antislavery.org/homepage/resources/cocoa%20report%202004.pdf, accessed on 25 September 2007.

Pearson, E. 2002. *Human Traffic, Human Rights: Redefining Victim Protection*. London, Anti-Slavery International.

Portes, J. and French, S. 2005. *The Impact of Free Movement of Workers from Central and Eastern Europe on the UK Labour Market: Early Evidence*. Leeds, Department for Work and Pensions. Available at http://www.dwp.gov.uk/asd/asd5/WP18.pdf, accessed on 30 October 2007.

Sen, S. (ed) 2004. *A Report on Trafficking in Women and Children in India, 2002-2003*. New Delhi, National Human Rights Commission. Available at http://www.ashanet.org/focusgroups/sanctuary/articles/ReportonTrafficking.pdf, accessed on 25 September 2007.

Sharma, B. 2006. *Contemporary Forms of Slavery in Brazil*. London, Anti-Slavery International. Available at http://www.antislavery.org/homepage/resources/PDF/Contemporary%20Forms%20of%20Slavery%20in%20Brazil.pdf, accessed on 25 September 2007.

Skrivánková, K. 2006. *Trafficking for Forced Labour: UK Country Report*. London, Anti-Slavery International. Available at http://www.antislavery.org/homepage/resources/PDF/Trafficking%20for%20Forced%20Labour%20UK%20Country%20Report.pdf, accessed on 31 October 2007.

Skrivánková, K. 2007. United Kingdom. *Collateral Damage: The Impact of Anti-Trafficking Measures on Human Rights around the World*. Bangkok, Global Alliance Against Traffic in Women, pp. 203-229. Available at http://www.gaatw.net/index.php?option=com_content&task=blogcategory&id=0&Itemid=179, accessed on 5 November 2007.

Slavery, Abduction and Forced Servitude in Sudan, Report of the International Eminent Persons Group. 2002. Available at http://www.state.gov/documents/organization/11951.pdf, accessed on 14 September 2007.

Slavery in Mauritania: Report on Field Research. 1992. London, Anti-Slavery International.

Slavery: Report prepared by Benjamin Whitaker, Special Rapporteur of the Sub-Commission on Prevention of Discrimination and Protection of Minorities, Updating the Report on Slavery Submitted to the Sub-Commission in 1966. United Nations, Economic and Social Council, E/CN/Sub.2/1982/20/Rev.1, 1982.

Souaré, I. 2007. *Mauritania: Criminalisation of Slavery is a Welcome Development, But…* Institute for Security Studies. Available at http://www.iss.co.za/index.php?link_id=4059&slink_id=4896&link_type=12&slink_type=12&tmpl_id=3, accessed on 29 October 2007.

Srivastava, R. 2005. *Bonded Labour in India: Its Incidence and Pattern*. Geneva, International Labour Office. Available at http://www.ilo.org/dyn/declaris/DECLARATIONWEB.DOWNLOAD_BLOB?Var_DocumentID=5071, accessed on 28 October 2007.

Steinfatt, T. Baker, S. and Beesey, A. 2002. *Measuring the Number of Trafficked Women in Cambodia: Part I of a Series*. Paper presented at conference on 'The Human Rights Challenge of Globalization in Asia-Pacific-US: The Trafficking in Persons, Especially Women and Children', Honolulu, 13-15 November.

Sunderland, J. and Varia, N. 2006. *Swept Under the Rug: Abuses against Domestic Workers Around the World*. New York, Human Rights Watch. Available at http://hrw.org/reports/2006/wrd0706/wrd0706web.pdf, accessed on 26 September 2007.

UNDP. 2008. *Human Development Report 2007/2008 – Fighting Climate Change: Human Solidarity in a Divided World*. 2008. New York, United Nations Development Programme. Available at http://hdr.undp.org/en/media/HDR_20072008_EN_Complete.pdf, accessed on the 21 August 2008.

United Nations. 1951. *The Suppression of Slavery*. United Nations, Economic and Social Council, Ad Hoc Committee on Slavery, U.Na. 275ST/SOA/A, 11 July, 1951.

United Nations. 1987. *Report of the Working Group on Slavery on its Twelfth Session*. United Nations, Economic and Social Council, E/CN.4/Sub.2/1987/25, 28 August 1987.

Varia, N. 2005. *Maid to Order: Ending Abuses Against Migrant Workers in Singapore*. New York, Human Rights Watch.

Weissbrodt, D. and Anti-Slavery International. 2002. *Abolishing Slavery and its Contemporary Forms*. New York, United Nations. Available at www.unhchr.ch/pdf/slavery.pdf, accessed on 2 September 2007.

Books and Articles

Applebaum, A. 2003. *Gulag: A History of the Soviet Camps*. London, Penguin.

Allain, J. 2006. Slavery and the League of Nations: Ethiopia as a Civilised Nation. *Journal of the History of International Law*, No. 8, pp. 213-244.

Allen, R. 2004. The Mascarene Slave-Trade and Labour Migration in the Indian Ocean during the Eighteenth and Nineteenth Centuries. G. Campbell (ed), *The Structure of Slavery in Indian Africa and Asia*. London, Frank Cass, pp. 33-50.

Anderson, B. 2000. *Doing the Dirty Work: The Global Politics of Domestic Labour*. London, Zed Books.

Anderson, B. 2004. Migrant Domestic Workers and Slavery. C. van den Anker (ed), *The Political Economy of the New Slavery*. Houndmills, Palgrave, pp. 107-117.

Andreas, P. 2001. The Transformation of Migrant Smuggling across the U.S.-Mexican Border. D. Kyle and R. Koslowski (eds), *Global Human Smuggling: Comparative Perspectives*. Baltimore, Johns Hopkins University Press, pp. 107-122

Anstey, R. 1968. Capitalism and Slavery: A Critique. *The Economic History Review*, No. 21, pp. 307-320.

Anstey, R. 1975. *The Atlantic Slave Trade and British Abolition*. London, Macmillan.

Bales, K. 1999. *Disposable People: New Slavery in the Global Economy*. Berkeley, University of California Press.

Bales, K. 2005. *Understanding Global Slavery: A Reader*. Berkeley, University of California Press.

Bales, K. 2007. *Ending Slavery: How We Free Today's Slaves*. Berkeley, University of California Press.

Bassiouni, C. 1991. Enslavement as an International Crime. *New York University Journal of International Law and Politics*, No. 23, pp. 458-517.

Beachey, R. 1976. *The Slave Trade of Eastern Africa*. London, Rex Collings.

Bethel, L. 1970. *The Abolition of the Brazilian Slave Trade: Britain, Brazil and the Slave Trade Question 1807-1869*. Cambridge, Cambridge University Press.

Berman, J. 2003. (Un)popular Strangers and Crises (un)Bounded: Discourses of Sex Trafficking, the European Political Community and the Panicked State of the Modern State. *European Journal of International Relations*, No. 9, pp. 37-86.

Berlin, I. 1998. *Many Thousands Gone: The First Two Centuries of Slavery in North America*. Cambridge, Massachusetts, Harvard University Press.

Blackburn, R. 1988. *The Overthrow of Colonial Slavery, 1776-1848*. London, Verso.

Blanchard, P. 2006. The Slave Soldiers of Spanish South America: From Independence to Abolition. C. Brown and P. Morgan (eds), *Arming Slaves: From Classical Times to the Modern Age*. New Haven, Yale University Press, pp. 255-273.

Blight, D. 2001. *Race and Reunion: The Civil War in American Memory*. Cambridge, Massachusetts, Harvard University Press.

Bloxham, D. 2001. Jewish Slave Labour and its Relationship to the 'Final Solution'. J. Roth, E. Maxwell, M. Levy, and W. Whitworth (eds), *Remembering for the Future, The Holocaust in an Age of Genocide*. New York, Palgrave, pp. 163-186.

Brantlinger, P. 2003. *Dark Vanishings: Discourses on the Extinction of Primitive Races, 1800-1930*. Ithaca, Cornell University Press.

Brooks, R. 2004. *Atonement and Forgiveness: A New Model for Black Reparations*. Berkeley, University of California Press.

Brown, C. 2006. *Moral Capital: Foundations of British Abolitionism*. Chapel Hill, University of North Carolina Press.

Brown, C. and Morgan, P. (eds). 2006. *Arming Slaves: From Classical Times to the Modern Age*. New Haven, Yale University Press.

Bush, M. 2000. *Servitude in Modern Times*. Cambridge, Polity Press.

Campbell, G. 2004. Introduction: Slavery and Other Forms of Unfree Labour in the Indian Ocean World. G. Campbell (ed), *The Structure of Slavery in Indian Africa and Asia*. London, Frank Cass, pp. vii-xxxii.

Carrington, S. 2002. *The Sugar Industry and Abolition of the Slave Trade 1775-1810*. Gainesville, University of Florida Press.

Chatterjee, I. 1999. *Gender, Slavery and Law in Colonial India*. Oxford, Oxford University Press.

Chatterjee, I. 2006. Slavery, Semantics and the Sound of Silence. I. Chatterjee and R. Eaton (eds), *Slavery and South Asian History*. Bloomington, Indiana University Press, pp. 287-315.

Cheah, P. 2006. *Inhuman Conditions: On Cosmopolitanism and Human Rights*. Cambridge, Massachusetts, Harvard University Press.

Chiang, C. 1994. Female Migrants in Singapore: Towards a Strategy of Pragmatism and Coping. M. Jaschok and S. Miers (eds), *Women and Chinese Patriarchy: Submission, Servitude and Escape*. London, Zed Books, pp. 238-263

Clarence-Smith, W. (ed) 1989. *The Economics of the Indian Ocean Slave Trade.* London, Frank Cass.

Clarence-Smith, W. 2006. *Islam and the Abolition of Slavery.* Oxford, Oxford University Press.

Cohen, D. and Greene, J. (eds) 1972. *Neither Slave Nor Free: The Freedmen of African Descent in the Slave Societies of the New World.* Baltimore, Johns Hopkins University Press.

Conklin, A. 1997. *A Mission to Civilize: The Republican Idea of Empire in France and West Africa, 1895-1930.* Stanford, Stanford University Press.

Cooper, F. 1977. *Plantation Slavery on the East Coast of Africa.* New Haven, Yale University Press.

Cooper, F. 1980. *From Slaves to Squatters: Plantation Labor in Agriculture in Zanzibar and Coastal Kenya, 1890-1925.* New Haven, Yale University Press.

Cooper, F. 2000. Conditions Analogous to Slavery; Imperialism and Free Labor Ideology in Africa. F. Cooper, T. Holt and R. Scott (eds), *Beyond Slavery: Explorations of Race, Labor, and Citizenship in Postemancipation Societies.* Chapel Hill, University of North Carolina Press, pp. 107-149.

Cotton, S. 1998. *Silent Terror: A Journey into Contemporary African Slavery.* New York, Harlem River Press.

Craton, M. 1982. *Testing the Chains: Resistance to Slavery in the British West Indies.* Ithaca, Cornell University Press.

Crawford, N. 2002. *Argument and Change in World Politics: Ethics, Decolonization, and Humanitarian Intervention.* Cambridge, Cambridge University Press.

Crone, P. 2003. *Slaves on Horses: The Evolution of the Islamic Polity.* Cambridge, Cambridge University Press.

Curtin. P. 1969. *The Atlantic Slave Trade: A Census.* London, University of Wisconsin Press.

Daniel, P. 1990. *In the Shadow of Slavery: Peonage in the South, 1901-1969.* Urbana, University of Illinois Press.

Davidson, J. 2005. *Children and the Global Sex Trade.* Cambridge, Polity Press.

Davidson, J. and Anderson, B. 2006. The Trouble with 'Trafficking'. C. van den Anker and J. Doomernik (eds), *Trafficking and Women's Rights*. Houndmills, Palgrave, pp. 11-26.

Davis, D. 1975. *The Problem of Slavery in the Age of Revolution: 1770-1823*. Ithaca, Cornell University Press.

Davis, D. 2006. *Inhuman Bondage: The Rise and Fall of Slavery in the New World*. Oxford, Oxford University Press.

Davis, R. 2004. *Christian Slaves, Muslim Masters: White Slavery in the Mediterranean, the Barbary Coast, and Italy, 1500-1800*. Houndmills, Palgrave.

Derrick, J. 1975. *Africa's Slaves Today*. New York, Schocken Books.

Deyle, S. 2006. New Edition. *Carry Me Back: The Domestic Slave Trade in American Life*. Oxford, Oxford University Press.

Deutsch, J. 2006. *Emancipation without Abolition in German East Africa, 1884-1914*. Oxford, James Curry.

Diallo, G. 1993. *Mauritania: The Other Apartheid?* Current African Issues, 16. Nordiska Afrikainstitutet.

Doomernick, J. 2004. Migration and Security: The Wrong End of the Stick? C. van den Anker (ed), *The Political Economy of the New Slavery*. Hampshire, Palgrave, pp. 37-52.

Drescher, S. 1977. *Econocide: British Slavery in the Era of Abolition*. Pittsburgh, University of Pittsburgh Press.

Drescher, S. 1986. *Capitalism and Anti-Slavery, British Mobilization in Comparative Perspective*. Oxford, Oxford University Press.

Drescher, S. 1988. Brazilian Abolition in Comparative Perspective. *The Abolition of Slavery and the Aftermath of Emancipation in Brazil*. Durham, Duke University Press, pp. 23-54.

Drescher, S. 2002. *The Mighty Experiment: Free Labor Versus Slavery in British Emancipation*. Oxford, Oxford University Press.

Dubois, L. 2004. *A Colony of Citizens, Revolution and Slave Emancipation in the French Caribbean, 1787-1804*. Chapel Hill, University of North Carolina Press.

Duffy, J. 1967. *A Question of Slavery*. Oxford, Clarendon Press.

Eaton, R. 2006. Introduction. *Slavery and South Asian History*, I. Chatterjee and R. Eaton (eds). Bloomington, Indiana University Press, pp. 1-16.

Eaton, R. and Chatterjee, I. (eds) 2006. *Slavery and South Asian History*. Bloomington, Indiana University Press.

Edwards, J. 1982. Slavery, the Slave Trade and the Economic Reorganization of Ethiopia, 1916-1935. *African Economic History*, No. 11, pp. 3-14.

Ehrenreich, B. and Hochschild, A. (eds). 2002. *Global Women: Nannies, Maids, and Sex Workers in the New Economy*. New York, Metropolitan.

Eltis, D. 1987. *Economic Growth and the Ending of the Transatlantic Slave Trade*. Oxford, Oxford University Press.

Eltis, D. 2000. *The Rise of African Slavery in the Americas*. Cambridge, Cambridge University Press.

Eltis, D. 2001. The Volume and Structure of the Transatlantic Slave Trade: A Reassessment. *The William and Mary Quarterly*, No. 58, pp. 17-46.

Eltis, D. Behrendt, S. Richardson, D. and Klein, H. (eds). 1999. *The Transatlantic Slave Trade: A Database on CD-ROM*. Cambridge, Cambridge University Press.

Eltis, D. and Richardson, D. 1997. The 'Numbers Game' and Routes to Slavery. D. Eltis and D. Richardson (eds), *Routes to Slavery: Direction, Ethnicity and Mortality in the Transatlantic Slave Trade*. London, Frank Cass, pp. 1-15.

Eltis, D. and Richardson, D. 2008. A New Assessment of the Transatlantic Slave Trade. D. Eltis and D. Richardson (eds), *Extending the Frontiers: Essays on the New Transatlantic Slave Trade Database*. New Haven, Yale University Press, pp. 1-60.

Engerman, S. 2007. Slavery, Freedom and Sen. K. Appiah and M. Bunzl (eds), *Buying Freedom: The Ethics and Economics of Slave Redemption*. Princeton, Princeton University Press, pp. 77-107.

Fehrenbacher, D. 2001. *The Slaveholding Republic: An Account of the United States Government's Relations to Slavery*. Oxford, Oxford University Press.

Ferrer, A. 2006. Armed Slaves and Anticolonial Insurgency in Late Nineteenth-Century Cuba. C. Brown and P. Morgan (eds), *Arming Slaves: From Classical Times to the Modern Age*. New Haven, Yale University Press, pp. 304-329

Frederick, J. 2005. The Myth of Nepal-to-India Sex Trafficking: Its creation, its Maintenance, and its Influence on Anti-trafficking Interventions. K. Kempadoo, J. Sanghera, and B. Pattanaik (eds), *Trafficking and Prostitution Reconsidered: New Perspectives on Migration, Sex Work, and Human Rights*. Boulder, Paradigm Publishers, pp. 127-147.

Finley, M. 1980. *Ancient Slavery and Modern Ideology*. London, Chatto & Windus.

Finley, M. 1964. Between Slavery and Freedom. *Comparative Studies in Society and History*, No. 6, pp. 233-249.

Fladeland, B. 1972. *Men and Brothers: Anglo-American Anti-Slavery Cooperation*. Urbana, University of Illinois Press.

Fogel, R. 1989. *Without Consent or Contract: The Rise and Fall of American Slavery*. New York, W.W. Norton.

Fogel, R. and Engerman, S. 1974. *Time on the Cross: The Economics of Negro Slavery, Volume One*. Boston, Little, Brown and Company.

Foner, E. 1983. *Nothing but Freedom: Emancipation and its Legacy*. Baton Rouge, Louisiana State University Press.

Gallagher, A. 2001. Human Rights and the New UN Protocols on Trafficking and Migrant Smuggling: A Preliminary Analysis. *Human Rights Quarterly*, No. 23, pp. 975-1004.

Genovese, E. 1976. *Roll Jordan Roll: The World The Slaves Made*. New York, Vintage Books.

Geggus, D. 1982. *Slavery, War, and Revolution: The British Occupation of Saint Domingue, 1793-1798*. Oxford, Clarendon Press.

Geggus, D. (ed). 2001. *The Impact of the Haitian Revolution in the Atlantic World*. Columbia, University of South Carolina Press.

Geggus, D. 2006. The Arming of the Slaves in the Haitian Revolution. C. Brown and P. Morgan (eds), *Arming Slaves: From Classical Times to the Modern Age*. New Haven, Yale University Press, pp. 209-252.

Gibney, M. Howard-Hassmann, R. Coicaud, J. and Steiner, N. (eds). 2008. *The Age of Apology: Facing Up to the Past*. Philadelphia, Pennsylvania University Press.

Gong, G. 1984. *The Standard of 'Civilization' in International Society*. Oxford, Clarendon Press.

Gordon, M. 1989. *Slavery in the Arab World*. New York, New Amsterdam.

Grant, K. 2005. *A Civilised Savagery: Britain and the New Slaveries in Africa, 1884-1926*. New York, Routledge.

Greendige, C.W.W. 1958. *Slavery*. London, George Allen & Unwin.

Gregor, N. 1998. *Daimler-Benz in the Third Reich*. New Haven, Yale University Press.

Hall, G. 2005. *Slavery and African Ethnicities in the Americas: Restoring the Links*. Chapel Hill, University of North Carolina Press.

Herbert, U. 1997. *Hitler's Foreign Workers: Enforced Labour in Germany Under the Third Reich*. Cambridge, Cambridge University Press.

Hicks, G. 1995. *The Comfort Women: Sex Slaves of Japanese Imperial Forces*. Singapore, Heinemann Asia.

Hochschild, A. 1998. *King Leopold's Ghost: A Story of Greed, Terror, and Heroism in Colonial Africa*. Boston, Houghton Mifflin Company.

Holt, T. 1992. *The Problem of Freedom: Race, Labor, and Politics in Jamaica and Britain, 1832-1938*. Baltimore, Johns Hopkins University Press.

Honwana, A. 2007. *Child Soldiers in Africa*. Philadelphia, University of Pennsylvania Press.

Howard-Hassmann, R. 2008. *Reparations to Africa*. Philadelphia, University of Pennsylvania Press.

Iadarola, A. 1975. Ethiopia's Admission into the League of Nations: An Assessment of Motives. *The International Journal of African Historical Studies*, No. 8, pp. 601-622.

Inikori, J. 2002. *Africans and the Industrial Revolution in England: A Study in International Trade and Economic Development*. Cambridge, Cambridge University Press.

Jennings, L. 2000. *French Anti-Slavery: The Movement for the Abolition of Slavery in France, 1802-1848*. Cambridge, Cambridge University Press.

Jok, J. 2001. *War and Slavery in Sudan*. Philadelphia, University of Pennsylvania Press.

Jok, J. 2007. Slavery and Slave Redemption in Sudan. K. Appiah and M. Bunzl (eds), *Buying Freedom: The Ethics and Economics of Slave Redemption*. Princeton, Princeton University Press, pp. 143-157.

Kapur, R. 2005. Travel Plans: Border Crossings and the Rights of Transnational Migrants. *Harvard Human Rights Journal*, No. 18, pp. 107-138.

Kaufmann, C. and Pape, R. 1999. Explaining Costly Moral Action: Britain's Sixty-year Campaign Against the Atlantic Slave Trade. *International Organization*, No. 53, pp. 631-668.

Keck, M. and Sikkink, K. 1998. *Activists Beyond Borders: Advocacy Networks in International Politics*. Ithaca, Cornell University Press.

Killingray, D. 1989. Labour Exploitation for Military Campaigns in British Colonial Africa. *Journal of Contemporary History*, No. 24, pp. 483-501.

Klein, H. 1986. *African Slavery in Latin America and the Caribbean*. Oxford, Oxford University Press.

Klein, H. 1999. *The Atlantic Slave Trade*. Cambridge, Cambridge University Press.

Klein, H. Engerman, S. Haines, R. and Shlomowitz, R. 2001. Transoceanic Mortality: The Slave Trade in Comparative Perspective. *The William and Mary Quarterly*, No. 58, 93-118.

Klein, M. 1993. Introduction: Modern European Expansion and Traditional Servitude in Africa and Asia. M. Klein (ed), *Breaking the Chains: Slavery Bondage and Emancipation in Modern Africa and Asia*. Wisconsin, University of Wisconsin Press, pp. 3-36.

Klein, M. 1998. *Slavery and Colonial Rule in French West Africa*. Cambridge, Cambridge University Press.

Klein, M. 2005. The Emancipation of Slaves in the Indian Ocean. G. Campbell (ed), *Abolition and its Aftermath in Indian Ocean Africa and Asia*. New York, Routledge, pp. 198-218.

Kloosterboer. W. 1960. *Involuntary Labour Since the Abolition of Slavery*. Leiden, E.J. Brill.

Kopytoff, I. and Miers, S. 1977. African 'Slavery' as an Institution of Marginality. S. Miers and I. Kopytoff (eds), *Slavery in Africa, Historical and Anthropological Perspectives*. Madison, University of Wisconsin Press, pp. 3-81.

Koser, K. 2001. The Smuggling of Asylum Seekers into Western Europe; Contradictions, Conundrums, and Dilemmas. D. Kyle and R. Koslowski (eds), *Global Human Smuggling: Comparative Perspectives*. Baltimore, Johns Hopkins University Press, pp. 58-73.

Kraay, H. 2006. Arming Slaves in Brazil from the Seventeenth Century to the Nineteenth Century. C. Brown and P. Morgan (eds), *Arming Slaves: From Classical Times to the Modern Age*. New Haven, Yale University Press, pp. 146-179.

Kumar, D. 1993. Colonialism, Bondage and Caste in British India. *Breaking the Chains: Slavery, Bondage, and Emancipation in Modern Africa and Asia*, M. Klein (ed). Madison, University of Wisconsin Press, pp. 112-129.

Law, R. (ed). 1995. *From Slave Trade to 'Legitimate' Commerce: The Commercial Transition in Nineteenth-Century West Africa*. Cambridge, Cambridge University Press.

Lasker, B. 1950. *Human Bondage in Southeast Asia*. Chapel Hill, University of North Carolina Press.

Le Breton, B. 2003. *Trapped: Modern-Day Slavery in the Brazilian Amazon*. London, Kumarian Press.

Lewis, B. 1990. *Race and Slavery in the Middle East*. Oxford, Oxford University Press.

Lovejoy, P. 2000. *Transformations in Slavery: A History of Slavery in Africa*. Cambridge, Cambridge University Press.

Lovejoy, P. 2004. Slavery, the Bilād al-Sūdān, and the Frontiers of the African Diaspora. P. Lovejoy (ed), *Slavery and the Frontiers of Islam*. Princeton, Marhus Weiner Publishers, pp. 1-30.

Lovejoy, P. 2005. *Slavery, Commerce and Production in the Sokoto Caliphate of West Africa*. Trenton, Africa World Press.

Lovejoy, P. and Hogendorn, J. 1993. *Slow Death for Slavery: The Course of Abolition in Northern Nigeria, 1897-1936*. Cambridge, Cambridge University Press.

Manning, P. 1990. *Slavery and African Life: Occidental, Oriental, and African Slave Trades*. Cambridge, Cambridge University Press.

Manning, P. 2007. Legacies of Slavery: Comparisons of Labour and Culture. M. Dias (ed), *Legacies of Slavery: Comparative Perspectives*. Newcastle, Cambridge Scholars Publishing, pp. 16-34.

Marques, J. 2006. *The Sounds of Silence: Nineteenth-Century Portugal and the Abolition of the Slave Trade*. New York, Berghahn Books.

Martin, M. and Yaquinto, M. (eds) 2007. *Redress for Historical Injustices in the United States: On Reparations for Slavery, Jim Crow, and their Legacies.* Durham, Duke University Press.

Meillassoux, C. 1991. *The Anthropology of Slavery: The Womb of Iron and Gold.* London, Athlone Press.

Miers, S. 1975. *Britain and the Ending of the Slave Trade.* New York, Africana Publishing Company.

Miers, S. 2003. *Slavery in the Twentieth Century.* Walnut Creek, Altamira Press.

Miers, S. and Roberts, R. Introduction. S. Miers and R. Roberts (eds), *The End of Slavery in Africa,* Madison, University of Wisconsin Press, pp. 3-68.

Miller, J. 1988. *Way of Death: Merchant Capitalism and the Angolan Slave Trade, 1730-1830.* Madison, University of Wisconsin Press.

Nainta, R. 1997. *Bonded Labour in India: A Socio-Legal Study.* New Delhi, Aph Publications.

Northrup, D. 1995. *Indentured Labor in the Age of Imperialism, 1834-1922.* Cambridge, Cambridge University Press.

Northrup, D. 2002. *Africa's Discovery of Europe, 1450-1850.* Oxford, Oxford University Press.

Nwokeji, U. 1998. The Slave Emancipation Problematic: Igbo Society and the Colonial Equation. *Comparative Studies in Society and History,* No. 40, pp. 318-355.

Ohadike, D. 1999. 'When the Slaves Left, Owners Wept': Entrepreneurs and Emancipation among the Igbo People. S. Miers and M. Klein (eds), *Slavery and Colonial Rule in Africa.* London, Frank Cass, pp. 189- 207.

O'Hear, A. 1997. *Power Relations in Nigeria: Ilorin Slaves and Their Successors.* New York, University of Rochester Press.

Ochsenwald, W. 1980. Muslim-European Conflict in the Hijaz: The Slave-Trade Controversy, 1840-1895. *Middle Eastern Studies,* No. 16, pp. 115-126.

Oldfield, J. 2007. *'Chords of Freedom': Commemoration, Ritual and British Transatlantic slavery.* Manchester, Manchester University Press.

Patnaik, U. and Dingwaney, M. (eds), 1985. *Chains of Servitude: Bondage and Slavery in India.* Madras, Sangam.

Patterson, O. 1982. *Slavery and Social Death: A Comparative Study*. Cambridge, Mass, Harvard University Press.

Patterson, O. 1991. *Freedom*. United States, Basic Books.

Pipes. D. 1981. *Slave Soldiers and Islam: The Genesis of a Military System*. New Haven, Yale University Press.

Prakesh, G. 1990. *Bonded Histories: Genealogies of Labor Servitude in Colonial India*. Cambridge, Cambridge University Press.

Price, R. 1979. Introduction: Maroons and their Communities. R. Price (ed), *Maroon Societies*. Baltimore, Johns Hopkins University Press, pp. 1-30.

Quirk, J. 2006. The Anti-Slavery Project: Linking the Historical and Contemporary. *Human Rights Quarterly*, No. 28, pp. 565-598.

Quirk, J. 2007. Trafficked into Slavery. *Journal of Human Rights*, No. 6, pp. 181-207.

Quirk, J. 2008. Ending Slavery in All its Forms: Legal Abolition and Effective Emancipation in Historical Perspective. *International Journal of Human Rights*, No. 13, pp. 529-554.

Rassam, Y. 1999. Contemporary Forms of Slavery and the Evolution of the Prohibition of Slavery and the Slave Trade Under Customary International Law. *Virginia Journal Of International Law*, No. 39, pp. 303-352.

Reidy, J. 2006. Armed Slaves and the Struggle for Republican Liberty in the U.S. Civil War. C. Brown and P. Morgan (eds), *Arming Slaves: From Classical Times to the Modern Age*. New Haven, Yale University Press, pp. 274-303.

Rice, A. 2003. *Radical Narratives of the Black Atlantic*. London, Continuum.

Richards L. 2000. *The Slave Power: The Free North and Southern Domination, 1780-1860*. Baton Rouge, Louisiana State University Press.

Richardson, D. Forthcoming. Involuntary Migration in the Early Modern World, 1500-1800. D. Eltis and S. Engerman (eds), *The Cambridge History of World Slavery*. Cambridge, Cambridge University Press.

Robinson, R. 2000. *The Debt: What America Owes to Blacks*. New York, Penguin.

Robertson C. and Klein. M. 1984. *Women and Slavery in Africa*. Madison, University of Wisconsin Press.

Ruf, U. 1999. *Ending Slavery: Hierarchy, Dependency and Gender in Central Mauritania*. Bielefeld, Verlag.

Scott, J. 1990. *Domination and the Arts of Resistance: Hidden Transcripts*. New Haven, Yale University Press.

Shelley, T. 2007. *Exploited: Migrant Labour in the New Global Economy*. London, Zed Books.

Sikainga, A. 1996. *Slaves into Workers: Emancipation and Labor in Colonial Sudan*. Austen, University of Texas Press.

Simon, K. 1930. *Slavery*. London, Hodder & Stoughton.

Smallwood, S. 2007. *Saltwater Slavery: A Middle Passage from Africa to American Diaspora*. Cambridge, Mass, Harvard University Press.

Stilwell, S. 1999. 'Amana' and 'Asiri': Royal Slave Culture and the Colonial Regime in Kano. S. Miers and M. Klein (eds), *Slavery and Colonial Rule in Africa*. London, Frank Cass, pp. 167-184.

Solow, B. 1993. Slavery and Colonization. B. Solow (ed), *Slavery and the Rise of the Atlantic System*. Cambridge, Cambridge University Press, pp. 21-42.

Steinfield, R. 1991. *The Invention of Free Labor: The Employment Relation in English and American Law and Culture*. Chapel Hill, University of North Carolina Press.

Temperley, H. 2000. The Delegalization of Slavery in British India. H. Temperley (ed), *After Slavery: Emancipation and its Discontents*. London, Frank Cass, pp. 67-92.

Thompson, J. 2002. *Taking Responsibility for the Past, Reparation and Historical Injustice*. Cambridge, Polity Press.

Tickner, H. 1974. *A New System of Slavery: The Export of Indian Labour Overseas 1830-1920*. London, Oxford University Press.

Tucker, L. 1997. Child Slaves in Modern India: The Bonded Labor Problem, *Human Rights Quarterly*, No. 19, pp. 572-629.

Turley, D. 2000. *Slavery*. Oxford, Blackwell.

Ubah, C.N. 1991. Suppression of the Slave Trade in the Nigerian Emirates. *The Journal of African History*, No. 32, pp. 447-470.

Upadhyaya, K. 2004. Bonded Labour in South Asia: India, Nepal and Pakistan. C. van den Anker (ed), *The Political Economy of the New Slavery*. Hampshire, Palgrave, pp. 118-136.

UNESCO. 2008a. Data Comparison Sheet #1 (v. 2), Worldwide Trafficking
    Estimates by Organizations. UNESCO Trafficking Statistics Project.
    Available at
    http://www.unescobkk.org/fileadmin/user_upload/culture/
    Trafficking/statdatabase/Worldwide_Estimates_Feb2008.pdf (p.123),
    accessed on 28 November 2008.

UNESCO. 2008b. *EFA Global Monitoring Report 2009. Overcoming Inequality:
    Why Governance Matters*. Paris, UNESCO. Available at
    http://unesdoc.unesco.org/images/0017/001776/177683e.pdf

Vink, M. 2003. 'The World's Oldest Trade': Dutch Slavery and Slave Trade
    in the Indian Ocean in the Seventeenth Century. *Journal of World
    History*, No. 14, pp. 131-177.

Walkowitz, J. 1982. Male Vice and Feminist Virtue: Feminism and the Politics
    of Prostitution in Nineteenth Century Britain. *History Workshop*,
    No. 13, pp. 77-94.

Wallace, E. 2006. *The British Slave Trade and Public Memory*. New York,
    Columbia University Press.

Watson, J. 1980. Slavery as an Institution: Open and Closed Systems.
    J. Watson (ed), *Asian and African Systems of Slavery*. Oxford, Basil
    Blackwell, pp. 1-15.

Waugh, L. 2007. *Selling Olga: Stories of Trafficking and Resistance*. London,
    Phoenix.

Williams, E. 1964. *Capitalism and Slavery*. London, André Deutsch.

Yoshimi, Y. 2001. *Comfort Women: Sexual Slavery in the Japanese Military
    During World War II*. New York, Columbia University Press.

Zilversmit, A. 1967. *The First Emancipation: The Abolition of Slavery in
    the North*. Chicago, University of Chicago Press.

Image credits

Page 17

Cane cutters in Jamaica (c. 1880). Photo held by Schomburg Center for Research in Black Culture.

Page 23

Plantation overseers punishing blacks. In: Debret, J. B. 1834-39. *Voyage pittoresque et historique au Brésil.* Paris, vol. 2, plate 25.

Page 35

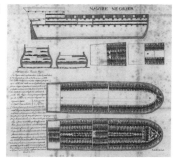

Slave ship. In: Société de la morale chrétienne, Comité pour l'abolition de la traite des Noirs. 1826. *Faits relatifs à la traite des Noirs.* Paris, fold-out facing title page.

Page 51

Down in the hold (1835). Painting by M. Rugendas.

Page 73

Toussaint Louverture (c. 1800). In: Rainsford, M. 1805. *An Historical Account of the Black Empire of Hayti.* London, facing p. 241.

Page 113

Primary school for freedmen, in charge of Mrs. Green, at Vicksburg, Mississippi (1866). In: *Harper's Weekly,* June 23, 1866.